Mometrix TEST PREPARATION

CPA

Business Environment & Concepts Exam

Secrets Study Guide

Dear Future Exam Success Story

First of all, **THANK YOU** for purchasing Mometrix study materials!

Second, congratulations! You are one of the few determined test-takers who are committed to doing whatever it takes to excel on your exam. **You have come to the right place.** We developed these study materials with one goal in mind: to deliver you the information you need in a format that's concise and easy to use.

In addition to optimizing your guide for the content of the test, we've outlined our recommended steps for breaking down the preparation process into small, attainable goals so you can make sure you stay on track.

We've also analyzed the entire test-taking process, identifying the most common pitfalls and showing how you can overcome them and be ready for any curveball the test throws you.

Standardized testing is one of the biggest obstacles on your road to success, which only increases the importance of doing well in the high-pressure, high-stakes environment of test day. Your results on this test could have a significant impact on your future, and this guide provides the information and practical advice to help you achieve your full potential on test day.

Your success is our success

We would love to hear from you! If you would like to share the story of your exam success or if you have any questions or comments in regard to our products, please contact us at **800-673-8175** or **support@mometrix.com**.

Thanks again for your business and we wish you continued success!

Sincerely,
The Mometrix Test Preparation Team

Need more help? Check out our flashcards at:
http://MometrixFlashcards.com/CPA

Written and edited by the Mometrix Exam Secrets Test Prep Team
Printed in the United States of America

TABLE OF CONTENTS

Introduction

Thank you for purchasing this resource! You have made the choice to prepare yourself for a test that could have a huge impact on your future, and this guide is designed to help you be fully ready for test day. Obviously, it's important to have a solid understanding of the test material, but you also need to be prepared for the unique environment and stressors of the test, so that you can perform to the best of your abilities.

For this purpose, the first section that appears in this guide is the **Secret Keys**. We've devoted countless hours to meticulously researching what works and what doesn't, and we've boiled down our findings to the five most impactful steps you can take to improve your performance on the test. We start at the beginning with study planning and move through the preparation process, all the way to the testing strategies that will help you get the most out of what you know when you're finally sitting in front of the test.

We recommend that you start preparing for your test as far in advance as possible. However, if you've bought this guide as a last-minute study resource and only have a few days before your test, we recommend that you skip over the first two Secret Keys since they address a long-term study plan.

If you struggle with **test anxiety**, we strongly encourage you to check out our recommendations for how you can overcome it. Test anxiety is a formidable foe, but it can be beaten, and we want to make sure you have the tools you need to defeat it.

Secret Key #1 – Plan Big, Study Small

There's a lot riding on your performance. If you want to ace this test, you're going to need to keep your skills sharp and the material fresh in your mind. You need a plan that lets you review everything you need to know while still fitting in your schedule. We'll break this strategy down into three categories.

Information Organization

Start with the information you already have: the official test outline. From this, you can make a complete list of all the concepts you need to cover before the test. Organize these concepts into groups that can be studied together, and create a list of any related vocabulary you need to learn so you can brush up on any difficult terms. You'll want to keep this vocabulary list handy once you actually start studying since you may need to add to it along the way.

Time Management

Once you have your set of study concepts, decide how to spread them out over the time you have left before the test. Break your study plan into small, clear goals so you have a manageable task for each day and know exactly what you're doing. Then just focus on one small step at a time. When you manage your time this way, you don't need to spend hours at a time studying. Studying a small block of content for a short period each day helps you retain information better and avoid stressing over how much you have left to do. You can relax knowing that you have a plan to cover everything in time. In order for this strategy to be effective though, you have to start studying early and stick to your schedule. Avoid the exhaustion and futility that comes from last-minute cramming!

Study Environment

The environment you study in has a big impact on your learning. Studying in a coffee shop, while probably more enjoyable, is not likely to be as fruitful as studying in a quiet room. It's important to keep distractions to a minimum. You're only planning to study for a short block of time, so make the most of it. Don't pause to check your phone or get up to find a snack. It's also important to **avoid multitasking**. Research has consistently shown that multitasking will make your studying dramatically less effective. Your study area should also be comfortable and well-lit so you don't have the distraction of straining your eyes or sitting on an uncomfortable chair.

The time of day you study is also important. You want to be rested and alert. Don't wait until just before bedtime. Study when you'll be most likely to comprehend and remember. Even better, if you know what time of day your test will be, set that time aside for study. That way your brain will be used to working on that subject at that specific time and you'll have a better chance of recalling information.

Finally, it can be helpful to team up with others who are studying for the same test. Your actual studying should be done in as isolated an environment as possible, but the work of organizing the information and setting up the study plan can be divided up. In between study sessions, you can discuss with your teammates the concepts that you're all studying and quiz each other on the details. Just be sure that your teammates are as serious about the test as you are. If you find that your study time is being replaced with social time, you might need to find a new team.

Secret Key #2 – Make Your Studying Count

You're devoting a lot of time and effort to preparing for this test, so you want to be absolutely certain it will pay off. This means doing more than just reading the content and hoping you can remember it on test day. It's important to make every minute of study count. There are two main areas you can focus on to make your studying count.

Retention

It doesn't matter how much time you study if you can't remember the material. You need to make sure you are retaining the concepts. To check your retention of the information you're learning, try recalling it at later times with minimal prompting. Try carrying around flashcards and glance at one or two from time to time or ask a friend who's also studying for the test to quiz you.

To enhance your retention, look for ways to put the information into practice so that you can apply it rather than simply recalling it. If you're using the information in practical ways, it will be much easier to remember. Similarly, it helps to solidify a concept in your mind if you're not only reading it to yourself but also explaining it to someone else. Ask a friend to let you teach them about a concept you're a little shaky on (or speak aloud to an imaginary audience if necessary). As you try to summarize, define, give examples, and answer your friend's questions, you'll understand the concepts better and they will stay with you longer. Finally, step back for a big picture view and ask yourself how each piece of information fits with the whole subject. When you link the different concepts together and see them working together as a whole, it's easier to remember the individual components.

Finally, practice showing your work on any multi-step problems, even if you're just studying. Writing out each step you take to solve a problem will help solidify the process in your mind, and you'll be more likely to remember it during the test.

Modality

Modality simply refers to the means or method by which you study. Choosing a study modality that fits your own individual learning style is crucial. No two people learn best in exactly the same way, so it's important to know your strengths and use them to your advantage.

For example, if you learn best by visualization, focus on visualizing a concept in your mind and draw an image or a diagram. Try color-coding your notes, illustrating them, or creating symbols that will trigger your mind to recall a learned concept. If you learn best by hearing or discussing information, find a study partner who learns the same way or read aloud to yourself. Think about how to put the information in your own words. Imagine that you are giving a lecture on the topic and record yourself so you can listen to it later.

For any learning style, flashcards can be helpful. Organize the information so you can take advantage of spare moments to review. Underline key words or phrases. Use different colors for different categories. Mnemonic devices (such as creating a short list in which every item starts with the same letter) can also help with retention. Find what works best for you and use it to store the information in your mind most effectively and easily.

Secret Key #3 – Practice the Right Way

Your success on test day depends not only on how many hours you put into preparing, but also on whether you prepared the right way. It's good to check along the way to see if your studying is paying off. One of the most effective ways to do this is by taking practice tests to evaluate your progress. Practice tests are useful because they show exactly where you need to improve. Every time you take a practice test, pay special attention to these three groups of questions:

- The questions you got wrong
- The questions you had to guess on, even if you guessed right
- The questions you found difficult or slow to work through

This will show you exactly what your weak areas are, and where you need to devote more study time. Ask yourself why each of these questions gave you trouble. Was it because you didn't understand the material? Was it because you didn't remember the vocabulary? Do you need more repetitions on this type of question to build speed and confidence? Dig into those questions and figure out how you can strengthen your weak areas as you go back to review the material.

Additionally, many practice tests have a section explaining the answer choices. It can be tempting to read the explanation and think that you now have a good understanding of the concept. However, an explanation likely only covers part of the question's broader context. Even if the explanation makes perfect sense, **go back and investigate** every concept related to the question until you're positive you have a thorough understanding.

As you go along, keep in mind that the practice test is just that: practice. Memorizing these questions and answers will not be very helpful on the actual test because it is unlikely to have any of the same exact questions. If you only know the right answers to the sample questions, you won't be prepared for the real thing. **Study the concepts** until you understand them fully, and then you'll be able to answer any question that shows up on the test.

It's important to wait on the practice tests until you're ready. If you take a test on your first day of study, you may be overwhelmed by the amount of material covered and how much you need to learn. Work up to it gradually.

On test day, you'll need to be prepared for answering questions, managing your time, and using the test-taking strategies you've learned. It's a lot to balance, like a mental marathon that will have a big impact on your future. Like training for a marathon, you'll need to start slowly and work your way up. When test day arrives, you'll be ready.

Start with the strategies you've read in the first two Secret Keys—plan your course and study in the way that works best for you. If you have time, consider using multiple study resources to get different approaches to the same concepts. It can be helpful to see difficult concepts from more than one angle. Then find a good source for practice tests. Many times, the test website will suggest potential study resources or provide sample tests.

Practice Test Strategy

If you're able to find at least three practice tests, we recommend this strategy:

UNTIMED AND OPEN-BOOK PRACTICE

Take the first test with no time constraints and with your notes and study guide handy. Take your time and focus on applying the strategies you've learned.

TIMED AND OPEN-BOOK PRACTICE

Take the second practice test open-book as well, but set a timer and practice pacing yourself to finish in time.

TIMED AND CLOSED-BOOK PRACTICE

Take any other practice tests as if it were test day. Set a timer and put away your study materials. Sit at a table or desk in a quiet room, imagine yourself at the testing center, and answer questions as quickly and accurately as possible.

Keep repeating timed and closed-book tests on a regular basis until you run out of practice tests or it's time for the actual test. Your mind will be ready for the schedule and stress of test day, and you'll be able to focus on recalling the material you've learned.

Secret Key #4 – Pace Yourself

Once you're fully prepared for the material on the test, your biggest challenge on test day will be managing your time. Just knowing that the clock is ticking can make you panic even if you have plenty of time left. Work on pacing yourself so you can build confidence against the time constraints of the exam. Pacing is a difficult skill to master, especially in a high-pressure environment, so **practice is vital**.

Set time expectations for your pace based on how much time is available. For example, if a section has 60 questions and the time limit is 30 minutes, you know you have to average 30 seconds or less per question in order to answer them all. Although 30 seconds is the hard limit, set 25 seconds per question as your goal, so you reserve extra time to spend on harder questions. When you budget extra time for the harder questions, you no longer have any reason to stress when those questions take longer to answer.

Don't let this time expectation distract you from working through the test at a calm, steady pace, but keep it in mind so you don't spend too much time on any one question. Recognize that taking extra time on one question you don't understand may keep you from answering two that you do understand later in the test. If your time limit for a question is up and you're still not sure of the answer, mark it and move on, and come back to it later if the time and the test format allow. If the testing format doesn't allow you to return to earlier questions, just make an educated guess; then put it out of your mind and move on.

On the easier questions, be careful not to rush. It may seem wise to hurry through them so you have more time for the challenging ones, but it's not worth missing one if you know the concept and just didn't take the time to read the question fully. Work efficiently but make sure you understand the question and have looked at all of the answer choices, since more than one may seem right at first.

Even if you're paying attention to the time, you may find yourself a little behind at some point. You should speed up to get back on track, but do so wisely. Don't panic; just take a few seconds less on each question until you're caught up. Don't guess without thinking, but do look through the answer choices and eliminate any you know are wrong. If you can get down to two choices, it is often worthwhile to guess from those. Once you've chosen an answer, move on and don't dwell on any that you skipped or had to hurry through. If a question was taking too long, chances are it was one of the harder ones, so you weren't as likely to get it right anyway.

On the other hand, if you find yourself getting ahead of schedule, it may be beneficial to slow down a little. The more quickly you work, the more likely you are to make a careless mistake that will affect your score. You've budgeted time for each question, so don't be afraid to spend that time. Practice an efficient but careful pace to get the most out of the time you have.

Secret Key #5 – Have a Plan for Guessing

When you're taking the test, you may find yourself stuck on a question. Some of the answer choices seem better than others, but you don't see the one answer choice that is obviously correct. What do you do?

The scenario described above is very common, yet most test takers have not effectively prepared for it. Developing and practicing a plan for guessing may be one of the single most effective uses of your time as you get ready for the exam.

In developing your plan for guessing, there are three questions to address:

- When should you start the guessing process?
- How should you narrow down the choices?
- Which answer should you choose?

When to Start the Guessing Process

Unless your plan for guessing is to select C every time (which, despite its merits, is not what we recommend), you need to leave yourself enough time to apply your answer elimination strategies. Since you have a limited amount of time for each question, that means that if you're going to give yourself the best shot at guessing correctly, you have to decide quickly whether or not you will guess.

Of course, the best-case scenario is that you don't have to guess at all, so first, see if you can answer the question based on your knowledge of the subject and basic reasoning skills. Focus on the key words in the question and try to jog your memory of related topics. Give yourself a chance to bring the knowledge to mind, but once you realize that you don't have (or you can't access) the knowledge you need to answer the question, it's time to start the guessing process.

It's almost always better to start the guessing process too early than too late. It only takes a few seconds to remember something and answer the question from knowledge. Carefully eliminating wrong answer choices takes longer. Plus, going through the process of eliminating answer choices can actually help jog your memory.

Summary: Start the guessing process as soon as you decide that you can't answer the question based on your knowledge.

How to Narrow Down the Choices

The next chapter in this book (**Test-Taking Strategies**) includes a wide range of strategies for how to approach questions and how to look for answer choices to eliminate. You will definitely want to read those carefully, practice them, and figure out which ones work best for you. Here though, we're going to address a mindset rather than a particular strategy.

Your odds of guessing an answer correctly depend on how many options you are choosing from.

Number of options left	5	4	3	2	1
Odds of guessing correctly	20%	25%	33%	50%	100%

You can see from this chart just how valuable it is to be able to eliminate incorrect answers and make an educated guess, but there are two things that many test takers do that cause them to miss out on the benefits of guessing:

- Accidentally eliminating the correct answer
- Selecting an answer based on an impression

We'll look at the first one here, and the second one in the next section.

To avoid accidentally eliminating the correct answer, we recommend a thought exercise called **the $5 challenge**. In this challenge, you only eliminate an answer choice from contention if you are willing to bet $5 on it being wrong. Why $5? Five dollars is a small but not insignificant amount of money. It's an amount you could afford to lose but wouldn't want to throw away. And while losing $5 once might not hurt too much, doing it twenty times will set you back $100. In the same way, each small decision you make—eliminating a choice here, guessing on a question there—won't by itself impact your score very much, but when you put them all together, they can make a big difference. By holding each answer choice elimination decision to a higher standard, you can reduce the risk of accidentally eliminating the correct answer.

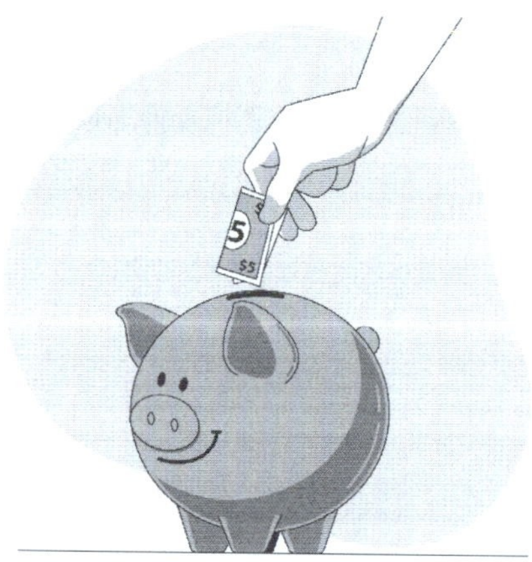

The $5 challenge can also be applied in a positive sense: If you are willing to bet $5 that an answer choice *is* correct, go ahead and mark it as correct.

Summary: Only eliminate an answer choice if you are willing to bet $5 that it is wrong.

Which Answer to Choose

You're taking the test. You've run into a hard question and decided you'll have to guess. You've eliminated all the answer choices you're willing to bet $5 on. Now you have to pick an answer. Why do we even need to talk about this? Why can't you just pick whichever one you feel like when the time comes?

The answer to these questions is that if you don't come into the test with a plan, you'll rely on your impression to select an answer choice, and if you do that, you risk falling into a trap. The test writers know that everyone who takes their test will be guessing on some of the questions, so they intentionally write wrong answer choices to seem plausible. You still have to pick an answer though, and if the wrong answer choices are designed to look right, how can you ever be sure that you're not falling for their trap? The best solution we've found to this dilemma is to take the decision out of your hands entirely. Here is the process we recommend:

Once you've eliminated any choices that you are confident (willing to bet $5) are wrong, select the first remaining choice as your answer.

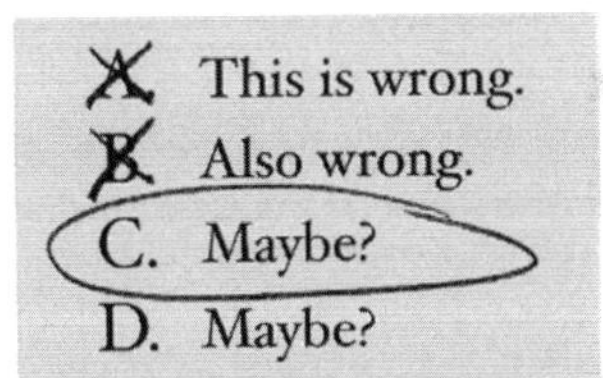

Whether you choose to select the first remaining choice, the second, or the last, the important thing is that you use some preselected standard. Using this approach guarantees that you will not be enticed into selecting an answer choice that looks right, because you are not basing your decision on how the answer choices look.

This is not meant to make you question your knowledge. Instead, it is to help you recognize the difference between your knowledge and your impressions. There's a huge difference between thinking an answer is right because of what you know, and thinking an answer is right because it looks or sounds like it should be right.

Summary: To ensure that your selection is appropriately random, make a predetermined selection from among all answer choices you have not eliminated.

Test-Taking Strategies

This section contains a list of test-taking strategies that you may find helpful as you work through the test. By taking what you know and applying logical thought, you can maximize your chances of answering any question correctly!

It is very important to realize that every question is different and every person is different: no single strategy will work on every question, and no single strategy will work for every person. That's why we've included all of them here, so you can try them out and determine which ones work best for different types of questions and which ones work best for you.

Question Strategies

✓ Read Carefully

Read the question and the answer choices carefully. Don't miss the question because you misread the terms. You have plenty of time to read each question thoroughly and make sure you understand what is being asked. Yet a happy medium must be attained, so don't waste too much time. You must read carefully and efficiently.

✓ Contextual Clues

Look for contextual clues. If the question includes a word you are not familiar with, look at the immediate context for some indication of what the word might mean. Contextual clues can often give you all the information you need to decipher the meaning of an unfamiliar word. Even if you can't determine the meaning, you may be able to narrow down the possibilities enough to make a solid guess at the answer to the question.

✓ Prefixes

If you're having trouble with a word in the question or answer choices, try dissecting it. Take advantage of every clue that the word might include. Prefixes can be a huge help. Usually, they allow you to determine a basic meaning. *Pre-* means before, *post-* means after, *pro-* is positive, *de-* is negative. From prefixes, you can get an idea of the general meaning of the word and try to put it into context.

✓ Hedge Words

Watch out for critical hedge words, such as *likely, may, can, often, almost, mostly, usually, generally, rarely,* and *sometimes.* Question writers insert these hedge phrases to cover every possibility. Often an answer choice will be wrong simply because it leaves no room for exception. Be on guard for answer choices that have definitive words such as *exactly* and *always.*

✓ Switchback Words

Stay alert for *switchbacks.* These are the words and phrases frequently used to alert you to shifts in thought. The most common switchback words are *but, although,* and *however.* Others include *nevertheless, on the other hand, even though, while, in spite of, despite,* and *regardless of.* Switchback words are important to catch because they can change the direction of the question or an answer choice.

⊘ FACE VALUE

When in doubt, use common sense. Accept the situation in the problem at face value. Don't read too much into it. These problems will not require you to make wild assumptions. If you have to go beyond creativity and warp time or space in order to have an answer choice fit the question, then you should move on and consider the other answer choices. These are normal problems rooted in reality. The applicable relationship or explanation may not be readily apparent, but it is there for you to figure out. Use your common sense to interpret anything that isn't clear.

Answer Choice Strategies

⊘ ANSWER SELECTION

The most thorough way to pick an answer choice is to identify and eliminate wrong answers until only one is left, then confirm it is the correct answer. Sometimes an answer choice may immediately seem right, but be careful. The test writers will usually put more than one reasonable answer choice on each question, so take a second to read all of them and make sure that the other choices are not equally obvious. As long as you have time left, it is better to read every answer choice than to pick the first one that looks right without checking the others.

⊘ ANSWER CHOICE FAMILIES

An answer choice family consists of two (in rare cases, three) answer choices that are very similar in construction and cannot all be true at the same time. If you see two answer choices that are direct opposites or parallels, one of them is usually the correct answer. For instance, if one answer choice says that quantity *x* increases and another either says that quantity *x* decreases (opposite) or says that quantity *y* increases (parallel), then those answer choices would fall into the same family. An answer choice that doesn't match the construction of the answer choice family is more likely to be incorrect. Most questions will not have answer choice families, but when they do appear, you should be prepared to recognize them.

⊘ ELIMINATE ANSWERS

Eliminate answer choices as soon as you realize they are wrong, but make sure you consider all possibilities. If you are eliminating answer choices and realize that the last one you are left with is also wrong, don't panic. Start over and consider each choice again. There may be something you missed the first time that you will realize on the second pass.

⊘ AVOID FACT TRAPS

Don't be distracted by an answer choice that is factually true but doesn't answer the question. You are looking for the choice that answers the question. Stay focused on what the question is asking for so you don't accidentally pick an answer that is true but incorrect. Always go back to the question and make sure the answer choice you've selected actually answers the question and is not merely a true statement.

⊘ EXTREME STATEMENTS

In general, you should avoid answers that put forth extreme actions as standard practice or proclaim controversial ideas as established fact. An answer choice that states the "process should be used in certain situations, if…" is much more likely to be correct than one that states the "process should be discontinued completely." The first is a calm rational statement and doesn't even make a definitive, uncompromising stance, using a hedge word *if* to provide wiggle room, whereas the second choice is far more extreme.

✓ Benchmark

As you read through the answer choices and you come across one that seems to answer the question well, mentally select that answer choice. This is not your final answer, but it's the one that will help you evaluate the other answer choices. The one that you selected is your benchmark or standard for judging each of the other answer choices. Every other answer choice must be compared to your benchmark. That choice is correct until proven otherwise by another answer choice beating it. If you find a better answer, then that one becomes your new benchmark. Once you've decided that no other choice answers the question as well as your benchmark, you have your final answer.

✓ Predict the Answer

Before you even start looking at the answer choices, it is often best to try to predict the answer. When you come up with the answer on your own, it is easier to avoid distractions and traps because you will know exactly what to look for. The right answer choice is unlikely to be word-for-word what you came up with, but it should be a close match. Even if you are confident that you have the right answer, you should still take the time to read each option before moving on.

General Strategies

✓ Tough Questions

If you are stumped on a problem or it appears too hard or too difficult, don't waste time. Move on! Remember though, if you can quickly check for obviously incorrect answer choices, your chances of guessing correctly are greatly improved. Before you completely give up, at least try to knock out a couple of possible answers. Eliminate what you can and then guess at the remaining answer choices before moving on.

✓ Check Your Work

Since you will probably not know every term listed and the answer to every question, it is important that you get credit for the ones that you do know. Don't miss any questions through careless mistakes. If at all possible, try to take a second to look back over your answer selection and make sure you've selected the correct answer choice and haven't made a costly careless mistake (such as marking an answer choice that you didn't mean to mark). This quick double check should more than pay for itself in caught mistakes for the time it costs.

✓ Pace Yourself

It's easy to be overwhelmed when you're looking at a page full of questions; your mind is confused and full of random thoughts, and the clock is ticking down faster than you would like. Calm down and maintain the pace that you have set for yourself. Especially as you get down to the last few minutes of the test, don't let the small numbers on the clock make you panic. As long as you are on track by monitoring your pace, you are guaranteed to have time for each question.

✓ Don't Rush

It is very easy to make errors when you are in a hurry. Maintaining a fast pace in answering questions is pointless if it makes you miss questions that you would have gotten right otherwise. Test writers like to include distracting information and wrong answers that seem right. Taking a little extra time to avoid careless mistakes can make all the difference in your test score. Find a pace that allows you to be confident in the answers that you select.

✓ KEEP MOVING

Panicking will not help you pass the test, so do your best to stay calm and keep moving. Taking deep breaths and going through the answer elimination steps you practiced can help to break through a stress barrier and keep your pace.

Final Notes

The combination of a solid foundation of content knowledge and the confidence that comes from practicing your plan for applying that knowledge is the key to maximizing your performance on test day. As your foundation of content knowledge is built up and strengthened, you'll find that the strategies included in this chapter become more and more effective in helping you quickly sift through the distractions and traps of the test to isolate the correct answer.

Now that you're preparing to move forward into the test content chapters of this book, be sure to keep your goal in mind. As you read, think about how you will be able to apply this information on the test. If you've already seen sample questions for the test and you have an idea of the question format and style, try to come up with questions of your own that you can answer based on what you're reading. This will give you valuable practice applying your knowledge in the same ways you can expect to on test day.

Good luck and good studying!

Corporate Governance

SHAREHOLDERS, THE BOARD OF DIRECTORS, AND OFFICERS

Shareholders have the right to corporation information; if shareholders have a proper purpose, they have the right to inspect the corporation books.

Shareholders must approve the following decisions: dissolution, mergers, charter or bylaw amendments, or sale of assets.

Corporations are generally run by a **board of directors**, who are elected by the shareholders. The board of directors is responsible for appointing officers of the corporation. The officers are responsible for running the daily business of the corporation.

BOARD OF DIRECTORS AND OFFICERS

AUTHORITY AND OBLIGATIONS

Any publicly-traded company is regulated by the SEC and required to have a **board of directors**, which have the authority and responsibility to oversee the company's operations, including not only its profit-generating strategy but its financial accountability to the public. Consequently, the board of directors ought to have a variety of people with expertise in financial reporting and in the business's operations, as well as an overall awareness of all the stakeholders' interests in the company's reporting and operations.

Officers hold similar levels of authority and responsibility. Major officers are generally appointed by an entity's board of directors. They can be officers and directors simultaneously, and they are also permitted to serve in more than one office.

AUDIT COMMITTEE

An **audit committee** is a committee independent of the corporation, but composed of board members, which is responsible for the audit work performed by the company's internal auditors and external auditors. Internal auditors have to directly report to the audit committee. At least one member of the audit committee must be a financial expert. Sarbanes-Oxley also establishes many regulations concerning the responsibilities and authority of audit committees.

DISCLOSURE COMMITTEE

Disclosure committees are not required to be formed, but are helpful in dealing with a company's disclosure issues. Such committees would help to determine the materiality of information and the applicability of certain disclosure requirements, improve company processes to ensure that quality information is disclosed in a timely manner, and assist with other disclosure issues. Disclosure committees typically report to the chief executives of the corporation.

EXTERNAL AUDITOR

COMPANY'S RESPONSIBILITIES

Since an external auditor ought to remain independent both in fact and in appearance, it is likewise vital that the company not compromise his independence in any way. This fundamentally involves the company taking responsibility for the appropriate activities and the external auditor taking responsibility for the appropriate activities. For example, the external auditor cannot be responsible about the effectiveness of the company's internal controls; that is the management's responsibility. According to the SEC, external auditors are permitted to gather information about a company, but management must direct the information-gathering process. If the auditor were solely in charge of both collecting information and appraising how well it was collected, it could too easily be interpreted as the auditor's auditing his own work.

Internal Control over Financial Reporting

Since the goal of internal controls is to ensure accuracy and completeness in financial reporting, there is always a tradeoff between the benefit of financial statement accuracy and the cost of implementing internal controls. This is the basis for objections against regulations proposed to mandate increased internal controls for companies with the intention of eliminating the chance of error or fraud in their financial statements. For example, resistance to Sarbanes-Oxley (2002) consisted of the fact that such heavy regulations were superfluous and would hinder business more than help it.

Aim of Internal Control

Internal control is the sum set of processes for a company which is designed to improve the company's objectives regarding the reliability of their financial statements, the efficacy and efficiency of their business activities, and the conformity of their practices with established legislation, with the emphasis especially placed upon financial statement reliability. Since the possibility of conspiracy, management override, or innocent errors in judgment or application may arise in any system, it is important to remember that the goal of internal control is not to eliminate all chances of error, but to reasonably limit them. Management is ultimately responsible for internal control effectiveness.

Committee of Sponsoring Organizations' (COSO) Integrated Framework

The **Committee of Sponsoring Organizations' (COSO) Institutional Framework** is a framework designed to improve, oversee, and maintain internal controls by emphasizing the most important features of a system of internal controls. These five COSO components are as follows:

1. the control environment, the foundation of the other four components, setting the tone of the organization;
2. risk assessment, which concerns the identification, evaluation, and management of risk;
3. information and communication;
4. control activities, which involve the policies ensuring that management decisions are carried out; and
5. monitoring, the process by which the quality of internal controls is monitored over time.

2013 Update to the COSO Integrated Framework

Since the first release of the COSO framework in 1992, many new changes have required an update for the framework in 2013. While the 2013 update was emphasized to be substantially similar to the 1992 original, such as in its central focus upon the five criteria of internal control, there are a few differences. The 2013 update offers the following:

- 17 explicit *principles*, each tied directly to one of the five criteria of internal control. This is the most significant change.
- 77 *points of focus*, each tied directly to one of the 17 principles.
- an updated discussion of technology: mobile devices, cloud-based systems, etc.
- an expanded description of and emphasis upon governance concepts, specifically that the oversight of the board of directors (including its various subcommittees) is vital to effective internal control

- a greater attention to fraud and its causes
- an increased focus upon non-financial reporting objectives, e.g. in improving internal operations and regulatory compliance

General Considerations of Internal Control

- There are inherent limitations to any system of internal control; no system can guarantee the impossibility of fraud or error. The best system can merely provide reasonable assurance.
- Smaller companies will have less flexibility to improve internal controls, especially with segregation of duties.
- Different controls have different relationships to different financial statement assertions. If the relation between some control and some assertion is more indirect, then that control should not be as much of a focus when attempting to reduce the control risk for the assertion.
- The cost of some internal control procedure ought not to outweigh the benefits.
- There should generally be routine controls for routine operations, and less routine controls for less routine operations.
- Controls can be manual or automated, and it is important that manual controls be tested more frequently.

Inherent Limitations of Internal Control

There are different ways in which internal controls are inherently limited. There can be different types of control deficiencies: design deficiencies (where a control fails to accomplish its objective even when running as designed) and operating deficiencies (where a control fails to operate as planned).

Internal controls can have material weaknesses, where there is a reasonable possibility that a material misstatement will occur. They can also have significant deficiencies, which are less severe than material weaknesses but still need correction.

Certain issues are matters of professional judgment, thus permitting a margin of error. This is especially true given the fact that many purely quantitative tests (such as when measuring materiality) are not acceptable, leading the auditors and management to also consider qualitative factors. These qualitative considerations include an appropriate consideration of unusual activity, the nature of the control environment, and many other things.

International Standards for the Professional Practice of Internal Auditing

The **International Standards for the Professional Practice of Internal Auditing** are standards issued by the Institute of Internal Auditors (IIA) and are intended to apply to internal auditing work without specifying such work to the diverse work environments in which it exists. The standards are focused on principles, meant to establish mandatory rules for the internal auditing practice and means of evaluating performance in a way that is internationally applicable.

The standards are composed of Attribute Standards and Performance Standards. The Attribute Standards concern the attributes of companies and persons who are performing internal audits, whereas the Performance Standards concern criteria for the evaluation of internal audits.

Sarbanes-Oxley Act (SOX)

Relevance to Internal Control

The Sarbanes-Oxley Act requires companies to establish and maintain an appropriate system of internal control.

Section 302 of the act requires a company's chief officers to review and certify the financial statements' accuracy, reliability, and completeness, as well as the internal controls' reliability and effectiveness. Signing officers have a very high liability according to SOX in order to motivate them to personally ensure the reliability of the controls and financial statement assertions.

-Section 404 demands that management also work for the implementation and maintenance of an appropriate control structure.

Section 302 Requirements

Section 302 of the Sarbanes-Oxley Act specifically focuses on a company's CEO and CFO, requiring them to be responsible for the company's implementation and maintenance of internal controls. They also must appraise the internal controls' effectiveness and present conclusions on them.

The officers are required to certify that they have reviewed the financial reports themselves, and that, as best as they know, the reports are materially accurate and fairly presented. A fair presentation of financial reports includes footnote disclosures and goes beyond the requirements of GAAP.

Section 404 Requirements

Section 404 of the Sarbanes-Oxley Act focuses on a company's internal control on financial reporting (ICFR). The section requires that management and the external auditor both validate the legitimacy of the client's ICFR. This section has been a very controversial part of the bill, since such validation is very expensive to carry out.

The management is required to issue an annual report on ICFR, a statement of responsibility for ICFR, a statement if conclusion regarding operating effectiveness of ICFR, and the disclosure of any material weaknesses. The external auditor is then required to report upon the management's evaluation of ICFR.

Enterprise Risk Management (ERM)

Enterprise risk management (ERM) is the company's overall approach to managing risk, taking into account the objectives to be achieved and the "risk appetite" which the company is willing to accept. There are four components to a company's risk strategy: risk avoidance (entirely forgoing an activity), risk reduction (establishing some control to mitigate the risk of some activity), risk sharing (splitting risk with another organization, e.g. a joint venture), and risk acceptance (embracing the risk in full, if the benefits outweighs the costs).

Components

The framework for enterprise risk management can be seen as an expansion of the COSO risk assessment component into three different components. These three components are the formulation of the organization's objectives, the specification of any events, internal or external, that could keep the company from attaining those objectives, and the choosing of a risk management strategy in relation to those events.

Control Environment

The **control environment** reflects the overall attitude, awareness, and actions of the board of directors, management, owners, and others concerning the importance of control and its emphasis in the entity.

Factors which collectively affect the control environment include:

1. Integrity and ethical values - code of conduct, use of appropriate incentive schemes
2. Audit committee and Board of Directors - oversee accounting policies and practices
3. Philosophy of management and operating style - attitude toward financial reporting, approach to risk
4. Assignment of authority and responsibility
5. Commitment to competence - ensuring competence, requisite skills, knowledge for particular jobs
6. Human resource policies and procedures - sufficient, competent personnel with adequate resources
7. Organizational structure - assigns authority and responsibility

Importance of a Corporate Culture for Internal Control

A corporate culture is crucially important for internal control, for it involves the general thought processes and motivations of all the workers in the company. If a company has and consistently enforces a code of conduct, has appropriate whistleblower procedures, facilitates training on ethical issues, and has other hedges in place to help motivate workers to avoid error and fraud, then the organization will have a much better chance of preventing material errors.

Factors of Monitoring Control Effectiveness

Design Effectiveness, Risk-Based Evaluation, Multiple Locations, Company-Level Controls, and Key Controls

Design effectiveness - The first step of monitoring control effectiveness should be to test the design effectiveness of company-level controls, examine and test financial statement assertions, and evaluate the processes leading to such assertions.

Risk-based evaluation - The prioritization of evaluating different elements of the financial statements should be according to the probability that such elements could cause a material misstatement.

Multiple locations - Controls do not need to be tested at every business unit for the company, although any units or locations left unassessed should be immaterial in importance.

Company-level controls - To the degree that company-level controls are not effective, the appraisal of operating controls at the level of business units or locations becomes necessary.

Key controls - Key controls are the most important controls in lowering the risk of material misstatement, fraud, or error. They should therefore be high-priority.

Monitoring Control Effectiveness,

Distinctions Among Primary, Secondary, and Tertiary Controls

Primary, secondary, and tertiary controls - Primary controls are most important for reducing the risk of material misstatement for some significant financial statement element. Secondary and tertiary controls are subsequently less important.

Company-level and process-level controls – Strong company-level controls work to reduce the necessity of process-level controls and of other testing.

Preventive and detective controls – A good internal control system should have both kinds of controls working in tandem to reduce the risk of material error. Preventive controls work before or during the inputting of a transaction, seeking to keep errors from occurring, whereas detective controls work after the inputting of a transaction for the timely detection of errors.

Manual and automated controls – It takes more time to properly test manual controls than automated controls, and any system of internal controls which is largely based on manual controls can face much difficulty under times of stress or change.

SAMPLING

Sampling is very important for monitoring control effectiveness as it seeks to conclusively establish the operating effectiveness of some control. A crucial element of sampling is the determination of the sample size, which determination depends upon the nature and surrounding circumstances of the control. For all sampling, management has the primary responsibility in discerning whether sufficient testing has been done to arrive at a conclusion of the reliability of the control.

CHANGE CONTROL PROCESS

The **change control process** works to identify and implement all necessary changes to internal controls for financial reporting. It is a formal process, not merely something that should happen incidentally. After identifying a problem and implementing a change in the control, the changed process needs to be tested and monitored appropriately.

ROLE OF THE AUDIT COMMITTEE

The audit committee provides oversight over the management for their identification and implementation of changes through the change control process. Since the audit committee is an independent party, it is well suited to provide oversight. The audit committee should have plenty of communication with management, internal auditors, external auditors, and others to ensure that management is doing an appropriate job with the change control process.

Economic Concepts and Analysis

Business Cycles

Business cycles are aggregate economic output changes that continue for an extended period of time. Business cycles continuously occur, though they differ in duration and strength. Business cycles are made up of peaks and troughs. A peak marks the end of an expansion and the beginning of a recession. A trough notes a recession's end and an expansion's beginning. During expansion, real Gross Domestic Product (GDP) goes up. As expansion reaches its climax, labor and materials are in short supply, causing inflation to begin. Recessions are typically made up of negative growth in GDP for two consecutive quarters. An intense ongoing recession is called a depression.

-Business cycles occur primarily due to business investment spending, as well as consumer spending for durable goods such as vehicles and household appliances. Some businesses are affected more than others during various business cycles. Cyclical businesses have better performance in times of expansion and have worse performance in times of recession. Businesses that perform better in times of recession are referred to as defensive businesses.

-Economic indicators are used to prepare forecasts of business cycles. These indicators may lead economic trends of the future, occur with economic trends, or follow economic trends.

Gross Domestic Product

An economy's annual aggregate output is measured by its **gross domestic product** (GDP), the total market value of all final goods and services produced within a country over a period of one year.

GDP is a monetary measure of the economy's output. To be sure that GDP reflects society's valuation of the economy's output, market prices are used as bases of output valuation. To avoid multiple counting, only the values of final goods are counted; the values of intermediate goods are contained in the value of final goods. National income measures include only the value added by each firm. The value of an economy's output is the sum of all of its "added values." Non-production transactions are excluded from GDP. There are two methods of computing GDP – the income approach and the expenditure approach.

GDP differs from **gross national product** (GNP), which is the dollar value of all goods and services produced in a nation's economy, including goods and services produced abroad.

GDP differs from **real GDP**, which is adjusted for inflation, and from **net domestic product** (NDP), which is GDP less depreciation.

Measuring Gross Domestic Product (GDP)

Labor Compensation, Rent, Interest, and Profits

Income (Output) Approach to Measuring GDP

Gross domestic product (GDP) is equivalent to the total income received by factors of production engaged in the process of production during a certain period, usually one year, and can be measured under the income approach by adding labor compensation (wages and salaries), rent, interest and business profits.

Labor compensation includes wages and salaries paid by businesses and the government to workers, in addition to all other benefit payments by employers, such as payments towards social security, pension funds, and health insurance.

Rent income consists of net rents received by landlords. Rents are paid by households, businesses, and government.

Interest income includes interest payments which households receive on bank deposits or bonds.

Profits can be classified into **proprietors' income** and **corporate profits.** Proprietors' incomes are reported with net profits. Corporate profits are corporations' net earnings after business expenses. Corporate profits are divided into three parts: corporate income taxes, distributed dividends, and retained (undistributed) profits. The sum of labor compensation, rents, interest, proprietors' income, and corporate profits equals **national income** (for example, all incomes earned from US supplied resources at home and abroad).

Price Elasticity of Demand

Price elasticity of demand measures how responsive the quantity demanded is to a change in product price.

Mathematically:

Price elasticity of demand = percentage change in quantity demanded / percentage change in price;

or

(change in quantity demanded / original quantity demanded)/(change in price / original price)

Cross-Price Elasticity of Demand

Elasticity refers to how responsive one variable is to another. **Cross-price elasticity of demand** measures the responsiveness of the quantity demanded of one good to a change in the price of another good in terms of percentages. Cross-price elasticities can be used to define the size of a market for antitrust purposes, to determine whether or not there is an adequate amount of competition to allow a merger between large firms in the same market to occur. Managers use cross-price elasticities to help make pricing and product design decisions. If cross-price elasticities are large, it is difficult for a firm to charge a price that is higher than its rivals. Thus a firm developing a new product or service may want to try different versions in test cases in order to find a niche in which cross-price elasticities are small.

Cross Price Elasticity = [% Change in Quantity Demanded of X]/ [% Change in Price of Y].

Cross-price elasticity is positive between substitutes and negative between complements (where one good is used with the other). Cross-price elasticities between complements indicate how strong a complementary relationship exists, which may impact marketing decisions and may suggest cooperative marketing strategies.

Price Elasticity of Supply

The **price elasticity of supply** measures how responsive the quantity supplied is to a change in product price.

Mathematically, price elasticity of supply equals the percent change in quantity supplied divided by the percent change in price.

This equals

{change in quantity/ [(original quantity + new quantity)/2]} /

{change in price/ [(original price + new price)/2]}

Supply is price elastic if a small change in price results in a relatively large change in quantity supplied. In this case, producers are very responsive to a change in the price of a good or service.

Determinants of Price Elasticity of Supply

The **adaptability** of the production process affects how responsive a firm can be to an increase in price. If the production process can easily be changed, then the size of the firm's response will be greater than when it takes years to change how it produces goods.

The amount of **time** firms have to respond to a price change affects the size of that response. For most goods, in the short run, sellers are limited to current production capacity. In the short run, supply tends to be price inelastic. In the immediate period, supply tends to be perfectly price inelastic; right now, a seller is limited to stock on hand and often is not able to offer any more for sale as a result of an increase in price. Given time, however, firms can expand their production capacity and produce a greater quantity of goods per period. In the long run, supply tends to be price elastic.

Income Elasticity of Demand

Income elasticity of demand measures the responsiveness of quantity demanded to changes in consumer (disposable) income. This information may be quite important for pricing decisions, and may help firms target their marketing decisions.

Income elasticity = [% change in quantity demanded of x]/ [% change in consumer incomes]

Inferior goods have a negative income elasticity of demand, meaning that as incomes rise, quantity consumed falls. These are sometimes referred to as countercyclical goods, because the demand for them rises when the economy is in a downturn (recession). Examples include generic goods, used clothing and cars, haircuts at beauty colleges, etc. Inferior goods are those goods that low-income people are forced by their conditions to consume, and which are dropped when their incomes rise.

Short-Run Costs

In microeconomics, the **short run** is the decision-making period during which at least one input is considered fixed. The fixed input is commonly considered to be some aspect of capital, such as the production facility, but may also be a normally variable input that is fixed because of production technology requirements or a contractual commitment (e.g., a facility lease) related to production. Short-run analysis is focused on a planning period in which some input is fixed and others are variable, and the manager is selecting levels of variable input and production output to optimize given the constraint of the fixed input. The actual time period that makes up the economic short run depends on how long the fixed input remains fixed. For example, a retail business whose primary fixed input in the short run is a building lease has a short-run planning horizon equal to the period of time remaining on the lease, which may be six months or two years. On the other hand, a utility with a new coal-fired electric generating plant faces an economic short run planning period that may span twenty years or more.

Long-Run Costs, Fixed Costs, and Variable Costs

The economic **long run** is a planning horizon that looks beyond current commitments to a future period in which all inputs can be varied. A typical long-run analytical problem is the decision of whether to adjust capacity, seek a larger (or smaller) facility, change product lines, or adopt a new technology. At any given time managers must be concerned with both short-run and long-run analysis.

Fixed costs do not vary with the volume of goods or services produced as output. Fixed costs are the costs associated with the fixed inputs that define the economic short run. Fixed costs are only relevant in the economic short run. Even if the firm temporarily shuts down, it still continues to incur the fixed cost expense. This is typical of capital loans or facility lease agreements.

Variable costs vary (usually directly) with the volume of goods or services produced as output, and can be avoided by a temporary shutdown.

Long-Run Cost Curves and Long-Run Average Costs

A **cost curve** is a graph showing the costs of production as related to total quantity produced. In the long run, all factors of production are variable, and companies can enter or exit any industry or market and produce any output level by employing the needed quantities of inputs (such as labor and capital) and incurring the costs of producing that output. A company will use the level of capital that can produce a given level of output at the lowest possible average cost.

The **long-run average cost curve (LRAC)** shows the per-unit cost of producing a good or service in the long run when all inputs are variable. The LRAC curve is U-shaped, reflecting economies of scale when negatively sloped and diseconomies of scale when positively sloped. It shows the minimum or lowest average total cost at which a company can produce any given level of output in the long run.

Demand Curve

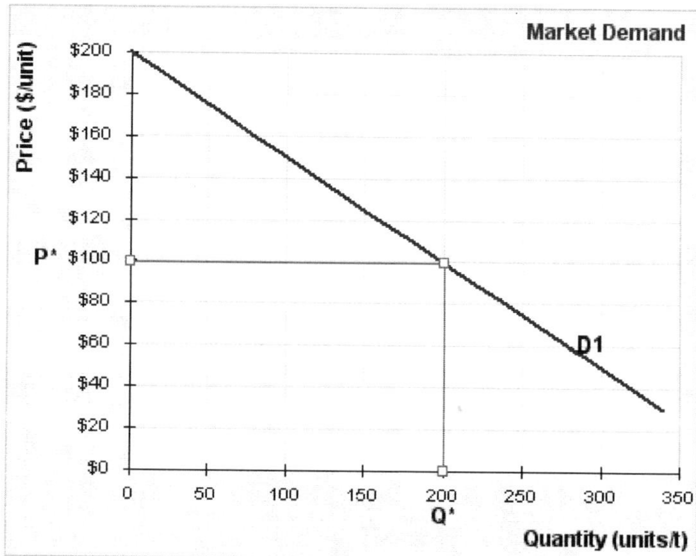

This demand curve (**D1**) depicts the **price** (in $ per unit) of a good buyers are willing to pay for a given **quantity** (in units per time period), everything else being held constant. There is an inverse relationship between price and quantity demanded.

SUPPLY CURVE

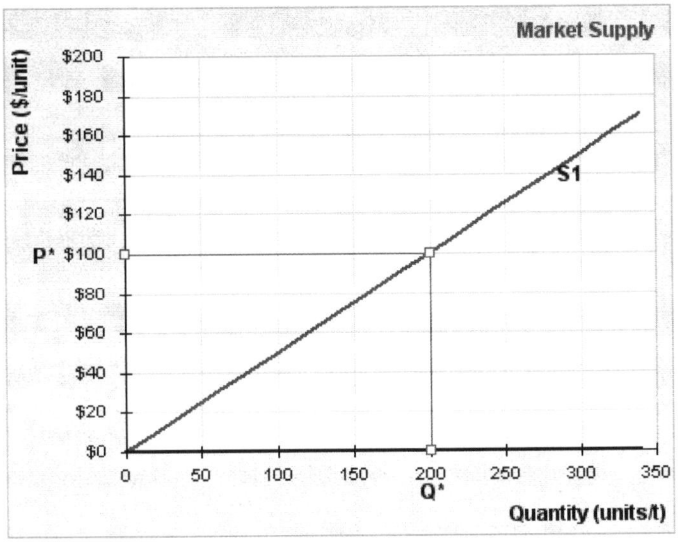

There is a direct relationship between quantity sold and price. This supply curve (**S1**) depicts the minimum **price** of a good sellers are willing to accept (in $ per unit) to offer a given **quantity** for sale during a specified period of time (units/t), everything else being held constant.

MARKET SUPPLY IN MICROECONOMICS

Seller reservation prices, or the minimum price at which a seller is willing to sell, vary, in part, due to differences in the costs of production. Some firms may be subsidized or taxed, face different prices for inputs, have different expectations regarding how demand for their product will change, or use different production technology. This indicates that the quantity of a good supplied by sellers varies with market price, all these other influences being held constant. As market price rises, more sellers will have a reservation price low enough to make the sale worthwhile. As price rises, producers can afford to employ more inputs and offer more of the good for sale. As price falls, fewer sellers will have a reservation price low enough to make the sale worthwhile. As price falls, producers cannot afford to employ as many inputs and will offer fewer units of the good for sale.

MARKET DEMAND IN MICROECONOMICS

The maximum price a buyer is willing to pay for one unit of a good or service, rather than do without, is called the **reservation price**. As a group, buyers' reservation prices for a given quantity of a good vary due to differences in the strength of their preference for the good, their knowledge of the price of substitute or complementary goods, their disposable income, and their expectations about what will happen to their income or the price of the good in the near future. This indicates that the quantity of a good demanded by buyers in a market varies with market price, all these other influences being held constant. As market price rises, fewer buyers will have a reservation price high enough to make the purchase worthwhile. That's because as price rises, good substitutes begin to look more attractive. As price falls, more buyers will have a reservation price low enough to make the purchase worthwhile. That's because as price falls, substitute uses for this good begin to look more attractive.

EQUILIBRIUM IN MICROECONOMICS

In microeconomics, **equilibrium** occurs when sellers and buyers both are able to optimize behavior. Sellers want to maximize profits and buyers want to maximize utility.

When quantity supplied by sellers equals the quantity demanded by buyers, equilibrium occurs; there is neither excess demand nor excess supply. Graphically, equilibrium is the point when the demand curve and the supply curve intersect.

The mathematical form of demand and supply equations can be used to calculate the equilibrium price and quantity.

In equilibrium, $\mathbf{Q_D\ (P^*) = Q_S\ (P^*)}$, i.e., neither a shortage nor a surplus exist at the equilibrium price, P*. To calculate that quantity, set Q_D (P) = Q_S (P) and solve for P: Q_D (P) = Q_S (P), where Q_D = quantity demanded, Q_S = quantity supplied, and P = price.

Excess Supply or Market Surplus

If the price of the good or service is higher than the equilibrium point, the quantity producers are willing to supply will exceed the quantity consumers are willing to purchase at the higher price, and a **market surplus** occurs. When quantity supplied exceeds quantity demanded, pressures in the market cause reductions in supply price and output to reach equilibrium.

Excess Demand or a Market Shortage

If the price of a good or service is lower than the equilibrium point, the quantity producers are willing to supply is less than the quantity consumers are willing to purchase at the lower price and a **market shortage** exists. For the market to reach equilibrium, a new equilibrium price and quantity under the new conditions must be reached.

Shifts in Demand and Supply

When the market adjusts to changes in the environment, supply and demand may change simultaneously, leading to a combined effect.

For instance, an increase in demand results in an increase in the equilibrium price, and an increase in supply results in a decrease in equilibrium price. When both supply and demand increases occur simultaneously, the actual impact on the equilibrium price depends upon the size of each of the changes.

To restore equilibrium after demand and supply change, price will have to be negotiated until quantity demanded and supplied is, once again, the same. Under conditions of both an increase in demand and a decrease in supply, the new equilibrium price will be higher than when either change is considered alone. The new equilibrium quantity, however, can be either larger or smaller than that at the initial equilibrium point, depending upon the relative size of the shifts in the two curves.

Effects of Government Price Controls

When price is free to move in response to the interplay of supply and demand, markets adjust to any change affecting the behavior of buyers and sellers. When the government regulates prices, the market does not function in the same way. For instance, when the government controls prices, some people are better off because they can buy a good or service at a lower price.

Governments can set prices by using price ceilings, which set the upper limit for a price, or price floors, which set the lower limit.

Price ceilings may cause suppliers to drop out of the market and new buyers to enter the market. In that case, demand exceeds supply, and a shortage occurs, which may result in rationing.

Price floors may mean that buyers reduce purchases because goods cost more, while suppliers increase production to take advantage of a higher price. This can cause excess supply. Price floors set above equilibrium prices can cause surpluses.

Price Ceilings

A **price ceiling** is a law requiring that a price for a certain good be kept below some level. The ceiling defines the maximum price that can be charged. Price ceilings can lead to shortages and a black market.

To be effective, the ceiling price must be set below the equilibrium price. A decrease in price causes an increase in the quantity demanded and a decrease in the quantity supplied. This creates a gap between the rising quantity demanded and the falling quantity supplied where none existed before (when the market was in equilibrium). This gap is called a shortage, resulting from excess demand.

Graph Reflecting the Effects of a Price Ceiling

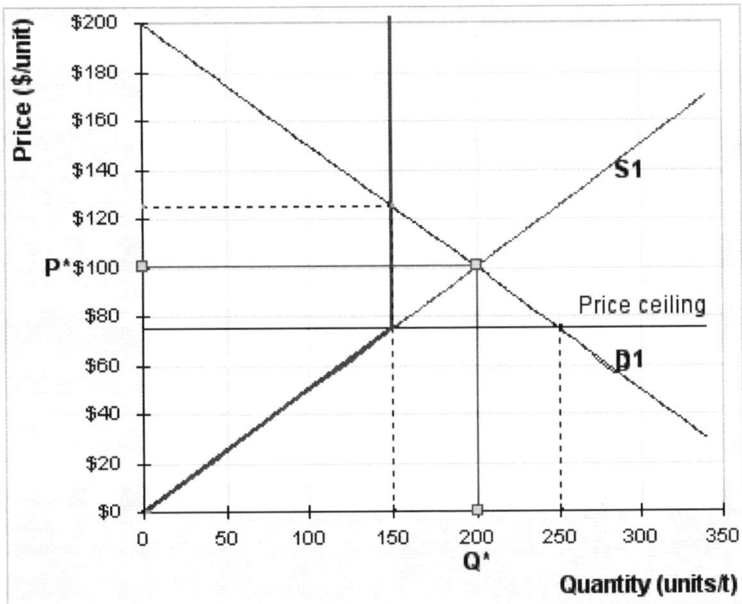

Unintended Consequences of Price Ceilings

Unintended consequences include rationing, which can happen when a price ceiling is set below equilibrium. This is because producers have no incentive to offer more goods, since the upper price limit is restricted, causing a shortage where buyers want more goods or services than are available.

Price ceilings may also cause a black market, which can happen when buyers are willing to pay more than the legally mandated price.

Consequences of Price Floors

Under normal market conditions, a market price that leads to a surplus would result in downward pressure on price. But when a price floor exists, because the lowest possible price is set by the government, firms cannot lower prices in response to the surplus. The surplus remains, and the government may have to step in to buy it.

PRICE FLOORS

A **price floor** is a government limit on how low a price can go. A price floor set above market equilibrium causes surpluses.

For example, suppose the government raises the minimum wage that may be paid to unskilled workers from the equilibrium wage of $100 per day to $125 per day. An increase in wages simultaneously causes a decrease in the quantity of labor demanded by firms and an increase in the quantity of labor supplied. This creates a gap between the falling quantity demanded and the rising quantity supplied where none existed before (when the market was in equilibrium); this gap is called a surplus.

OLIGOPOLIES AND MONOPOLISTIC COMPETITION

An **oligopoly** is a small number of firms controlling all or most sales. An example of an oligopolistic industry would be the airline industry. Businesses in an oligopoly usually avoid price competition. In an oligopoly, there are barriers to entry; it is challenging for a new firm to enter the industry. Advertising is typically done on a national level. Businesses in an oligopoly are usually interdependent. Unregulated oligopolies tend to form cartels, which create collusion among producers and retailers. Cartels are illegal in the United States but exist internationally.

Monopolistic competition occurs when a large number of firms sell products that are close substitutes, even though the products might have some differences. An example of a monopolistic competition industry would be retail stores. In monopolistic competition, it is easy for firms to enter or exit the industry. Advertising is typically done on a local level.

An industry's competitive market dictates the level of competition and threats to new firms attempting to enter the industry. Businesses are also affected by the possibility of substitute products being introduced to the market, as well as the bargaining power of customers and suppliers.

PERFECT COMPETITION AND PURE MONOPOLY

Perfect competition occurs when many small firms produce the same product, none of which can influence prices. In perfect competition, products among firms are identical, and there are no barriers to entry or to exit. There are no price controls or restrictions on production, and market price is determined by supply and demand.

A **pure monopoly** exists when a single firm produces a unique good for which there are no substitutes. New entries to the industry are not permitted, and the monopoly sets the prices. Monopolies result due to the following circumstances: government franchises (such as public utilities), exclusive patent rights, and control over raw material supplies.

INDIFFERENCE CURVES, PRICE ELASTICITY, REVENUE RELATIONSHIPS, AND MARGINAL UTILITY

The **indifference curve** is a line drawn through various combinations and quantities of the consumption alternatives that yield the same total utility.

When demand is **price inelastic**, quantity demanded is not very responsive to a given change in price. A producer can raise price and increase total revenue when demand is price inelastic. The opposite is true when demand is **price elastic**.

Marginal utility is the amount of increase (or decrease) in total utility that derives from consuming another unit of some particular good or service.

Inflation

Demand-Pull Inflation and Cost-Push Inflation

The **inflation** rate is the percentage change in the price level. Inflation can result from either an increase in aggregate demand or a decrease in aggregate supply.

Demand-pull inflation results from an initial increase in aggregate demand. Demand-pull inflation may begin with any factor that increases aggregate demand. Two factors controlled by the government are increases in the quantity of money and increases in government purchases. A third possibility is an increase in exports. Real gross domestic product (GDP) increases, the price level rises, and an inflationary gap arise. The rising price level is the first step in demand-pull inflation. Although any of several factors can increase aggregate demand to start demand-pull inflation, only an ongoing increase in the quantity of money can sustain it.

Cost-push inflation results from an initial increase in costs. There are two main sources of increased costs: a money wage rate increase or a raw material price increase. Stagflation occurs, which is the state of a decrease in real GDP and an increase in the price level. The rising price level is the start of cost-push inflation. The initial increase in costs creates a one-time rise in the price level, not inflation.

Types of Mergers

Horizontal mergers are between companies selling similar products in the same market, while **vertical mergers** are between firms at different stages of the production process in the same industry. **Conglomerate mergers** are between firms in unrelated industries.

Companies that are considering acquiring other companies use different ways of valuing the other companies, including the market multiple method and discounted cash flow analysis. The market multiple method assigns a multiple determined by the market to an earnings indicator, such as earnings per share or profit. A discounted cash flow analysis uses capital budgeting methods.

Basics of Globalization

Globalization is the process by which different nations, especially companies from different nations, are further integrated and interconnected. It has especially arisen in the last century with the vast improvements of transportation, telecommunications, and other technologies. Proponents of globalization promote it since they believe it helps to improve the world's overall wealth in the long run, facilitating trade according to each country's comparative advantage. Opponents of globalization see it as detrimental to local economies, since the outsourcing done by corporations amounts to an evacuation of wealth.

Shifts in Economic Balance of Power

The process of globalization naturally involves a movement of capital (economic balance of power) between developed and emerging or developing markets. This is often driven by corporations' desire for cheaper costs. For example, if a manufacturing corporation can employ cheaper labor costs and avoid various environmental regulations by outsourcing the manufacturing process to another nation, it will often do so, selling the manufactured goods back to consumers in the home nation. Consumers will then enjoy cheaper goods even though the manufacturing capital was moved to a separate nation. This is one way in which economic power is shifted from a developed to an emerging market.

Strategic Planning

SWOT Analysis, Product Differentiation, and Supply Chain Management

Strategic planning is the creation of long-term plans that help a company move from "where they are" to "where they want to be."

SWOT analysis is the assessment of strengths, weaknesses, opportunities, and threats. Businesses attempt to maintain and build strengths, using them as leverage, and will try to correct or get rid of any existing weaknesses. Opportunities are prioritized and optimized, and firms attempt to counter threats.

Product differentiation refers to how companies may compete by changing the characteristics of the product they sell. The idea is not necessarily to make a better product than the competitor, just a different one – to appeal to a different "market niche." Product differentiation increases variety, thus increasing the range of consumer choice, which is good; but it divides up the market, leading to higher prices and costs.

Supply chain management is the utilization of the supply chain to create opportunities for improvement by reducing timing, costs, and defects that take place as goods or services move from beginning to end of the manufacturing process.

Market Influences on Business Strategies

Market influences alter business strategies by informing businesses of which market niches they ought to pursue and by helping businesses compare their strengths, weaknesses, opportunities, and threats to competitors. Products typically have their own "life cycle," whereby they attain a certain peak level of popularity and then wane; it is therefore important for companies to predict this and get their products to the appropriate market segments in order to maximize profitability. Companies need to ensure that the demand for their products remains high.

Financial Risk Management

Financial risk management is the utilization of various financial instruments to handle risk for a business, especially credit risk and market risk. Financial risk management focuses on when to hedge and how to hedge different types of risks, including risks arising from inflation, liquidity, and foreign exchanges.

Risks

Inflation Risk, Business Cycle Risk, Interest Rate Risk, Management Risk, Business Risk, and Financial Risk

The more variable an investment's return, the greater its **risk**. A highly variable return could lead to investment losses if the investment needs to be sold. However, the longer the investment is held, the greater the chances of earning the long-run rate of return. Risk can be caused by changes in economic conditions.

Inflation risk occurs when there is an increase in inflation, and investment returns do not keep pace with the inflation increase.

Business cycle risk occurs when an investment return fluctuates in accordance with the overall business cycle.

Interest rate risk occurs when newly-issued bonds offer higher rates than bonds already being held.

Risk can be caused by changes in the security issuer's conditions.

Management risk is caused due to the possibility that a company in which an investor has invested has management issues.

Business risk occurs from risks associated with a company's product/service lines.

Financial risk may result from the risk of insolvency when a company has too much debt.

Investment risk premium – The return on US Treasury Bills (T-Bills) is risk-free. Any return greater than a T-bill return is the investment risk premium. Diversification reduces investment risk.

CASH AND LIQUIDITY MANAGEMENT

Cash and liquidity management involves forecasting a company's cash needs and managing cash flows, short-term borrowings, and cash in the most efficient manner to ensure those cash needs are met. Cash management involves establishing good banking relationships and maintaining control over receivables and payables in order to be able to predict cash flows and cash flow cycles.

Examples of cash management strategies include establishing a line of credit to avoid overdraft fees, using lockboxes to speed collection of receivables, zero balance accounts to reduce idle cash balances, and investment sweep accounts to earn interest by depositing excess funds in an overnight investment account.

ASPECTS OF CASH MANAGEMENT

FLOAT, ZERO BALANCE ACCOUNTS, AND LOCKBOXES

The **float** is the difference between the available or collected balance according to the bank and the company's book or ledger balance. When a check is written, the book or ledger balance is decreased by the check amount, but the available or collected balance at the bank is not decreased until the check clears the bank. This difference is called "disbursement float." Upon a company's receipt of a check payment, until the funds are credited to the company's bank account, the book balance will be higher than the company's actual balance. This float is called "collection float."

Zero balance accounts are unique disbursement accounts with a balance of zero that are funded from a master account. When checks are written on a zero balance account, the necessary funds are simultaneously transferred into the account. By centralizing payables, a cash manager knows when all bills must be paid and can make sure that funds are available and bills are paid on time.

Lockboxes are post office boxes to which a firm directs incoming checks. A bank is engaged to open the lockbox several times per day, process the checks, and collect them. This speeds up the collection process (and shortens the collection float).

ATTITUDES TOWARDS RISK

RISK-NEUTRAL, RISK-SEEKING, AND RISK AVERSE, MARKET RISK, CREDIT RISK, AND INTEREST RATE RISK

Risk-neutral investors seek higher-return investments without consideration for risk.

Risk-seeking investors search for investments with high risk, even if the same return can be earned for an investment with lower risk. Most investors are considered to be **risk averse**, meaning they will take risk if they receive adequate compensation in return.

Risk and Interest Rates

To determine an acceptable level of interest rates, business risks are reviewed. Business risks include market risk, credit risk, and interest rate risk.

Market risk is the risk that the principal value will decrease as a result of a decrease in value of the market.

Credit risk is the risk that the debtor will go into default on payments.

Interest rate risk is the risk that the principal value will decrease as a result of interest rates increasing.

Derivative Securities

Swaps, Futures and Forwards, and Spot Contracts

Derivative securities, which are securities whose value depends on the value of an underlying commodity or security, help hedge, or reduce, risk exposures. Misuse of derivatives can increase risk.

Swaps are agreements between parties to exchange future cash flows.

Futures and **forwards** represent agreements to buy or sell an underlying asset in the future for a specified price. Both provide price exposure without having to pay for, hold, or warehouse the underlying asset. Futures are traded on exchanges, while forwards trade over the counter.

A **spot contract** is an agreement for immediate delivery of a commodity and immediate payment for the commodity.

Fair Value Hedges, Cash Flow Hedges, and Net Investment Hedges

Fair value hedges offset the price risk of changes in value of a recognized asset or liability or unrecognized firm commitment.

Cash flow hedges offset the variability of the cash flow of a balance sheet item or a forecasted transaction.

Net investment hedges pertain to hedges of the net investment in a foreign operation.

While the accounting for these hedge relationships may vary, the following guidelines usually apply:

- For fair value hedges, the derivatives are marked to market in earnings. The value of the hedge will be offset by changes in the value of the underlying exposure.
- For cash flow hedges, the derivatives are marked to market and carried at fair value. The effective portion is recorded in other comprehensive income. The ineffective portion goes into current income.
- For net investment hedges, gains/losses in the hedge are recorded in other comprehensive income. Net investment hedges are currency-related and are a FAS 52 relic. Consequently, these hedges are inconsistent with much of the new derivatives accounting rule. For example, they allow companies to use nonderivatives (e.g. foreign currency borrowing) to cover their investment risk.

Financial Management

Quantitative Methods of Forecasting

Quantitative forecasting methods typically use some type of mathematical formula. The forecasting method chosen may depend on the time frame, supply or demand behavior, and causes of the supply or demand behavior. Other forecasting methods include time series methods or regression analysis methods.

- The **moving average** includes weighted moving average, simple moving average, and the naïve forecast. The simple moving average is based on steady activity with no distinct patterns of behavior.
- With the **naïve forecast**, the present period's activity is used as the prediction for the next period's activity.
- With the **weighted moving average**, weights are assigned to the most current data.

Exponential smoothing uses an averaging method with stronger weights on the most current data; this method reacts more to recent changes.

- One regression forecasting method is **linear regression**, which is a mathematical technique that reflects a relationship between a dependent variable and an independent variable in the form of a linear equation, such as y = a + bx + e, where a is the y-intercept, b is the regression line slope, e is the error term, x is the independent variable, and y is the dependent variable.

Calculating Present Value

Present value is the value in today's dollars of a sum of money to be received in the future. Present value results when the opportunity cost of having to wait for future consumption is factored into the amount to be received in the future. Mathematically, the present value of a sum of money to be received in the future can be determined with:

$$PV = FV_n\left(\frac{1}{(1+i)^n}\right)$$

$PV = FV(PVIF_{i,n})$ –By the use of Financial Tables on Present value

where: n = the number of years until payment will be received,

i = the opportunity rate or discount rate

PV = the present value of the future sum of money

FV_n = the future value of the investment at the end of n years

$PVIF_{i,n}$ = Present Value Interest Factor

Present Value of a Future Sum of Money

The present value of a future sum of money is the estimated worth today of an amount to be received or paid sometime in the future. Present value is inversely related to both the number of years until the payment will be received and the opportunity rate. At a positive rate of interest, present value will be less than future value with the difference reflecting the opportunity cost of funds given up.

Future Value

Future value is the estimated future worth of a sum on hand today invested at a fixed interest rate. Future value reflects appreciation of a present lump sum over time so as to return to the lender principal plus interest. Money has future value, because resources relinquished today will grow at the real rate which lenders require to forego present consumption.

Portfolio Returns

Factors That Cause Fluctuations

Portfolio returns fluctuate due to each asset's weight. or the portfolio percentage invested in each asset; due to each asset's return variance; and due to the asset returns' covariance.

-Sometimes, entities will base expected returns on historical trends. To compute the average historical return for a comparable investment, the following methods are sometimes used:

Arithmetic average return: usually used for assets with short holding periods.

(rate of return for year 1 + rate of return for year 2) / 2

Geometric average return: usually used for assets with long holding periods; this examines the compound annual return.

(capital / return) ^ (1 / n) – 1

where n = number of years

Liquidity Ratios and Profitability Ratios

Liquidity ratios measure the ability of a company to pay currently maturing debts.

Common liquidity ratios and the formulas for calculating them include:

1. Accounts receivable turnover = total credit sales / average accounts receivable
2. Accounts payable turnover = total credit purchases / average accounts payable
3. Inventory turnover = total cost of sales / average inventory
4. Acid-test = (cash + securities + accounts receivable) / current liabilities
5. Current ratio = current assets / current liabilities
6. Working capital = current assets – current liabilities

Profitability ratios measure how well management uses company resources to earn a return on investment. Examples of profitability ratios are profit margin, return on assets, and return on equity.

Expected Return on a Portfolio

Systematic Risk, the Risk-Free Rate, and the Market Risk Premium

The equation for the expected return on a portfolio gives the theoretically correct required rate of return on a project based upon its **systematic** (or beta) risk. The formula is applicable only in situations where all diversifiable risk has been eliminated. The required return on a project is positively related to the project's beta.

The **risk-free rate** is a base rate reflecting the fact that the project should, at a minimum, offer a return equal to what could be earned in the treasury bill market. Even riskless investments have a positive required rate of return.

The **market risk premium** indicates what the premium investors require over the risk-free rate. A very risky project (e.g. a new expansion venture) will have a high beta coefficient, whereas low-risk projects (e.g. a replacement machine) will have a lower beta. Knowing a project's beta (and thus its minimum required return) is important for good financial management, because it indicates whether or not the expected rate of return is above, equal to, or below the required rate of return and whether or not stockholders are being properly compensated for the non-diversifiable risk they bear due to the project.

Ratios

Coverage, Activity, and Debt

Coverage ratios involve the measure of security for long-term investors/creditors.

Activity ratios measure effective use of assets.

1. Accounts receivable turnover: average gross receivables / (net credit sales/365)
2. Inventory turnover: cost of goods sold / average inventory

Debt ratios measure the ability of a company's cash flows to meet debt obligations

1. Debt to equity: total debt / total equity
2. Debt to total assets: total debt / total assets

Decision Analysis

Opportunity Costs, Explicit Costs and Implicit Costs, Incremental and Sunk Costs

The **opportunity cost** of an asset (or, more generally, of a choice) is the highest valued opportunity that must be dismissed to allow current use.

Explicit costs are expenses which must be paid for with cash or cash equivalents. Because a cash transaction is involved, they are relatively easily accounted for in analysis.

Implicit costs do not involve a cash transaction, and so the opportunity cost concept is used to measure them. This analysis requires detailed knowledge of alternatives that were not selected at various decision points. Relevant here is the opportunity cost of the firm's assets and cash, and of the owner's time invested in the firm.

Incremental cost is the change in cost caused by a particular managerial decision. Thus the increment is at the decision level, and may involve multiple units of change in output or input. Incremental costs may be involved when considering a product or service modification or a change in production process.

Sunk costs are those parts of the purchase cost that cannot later be salvaged or modified through resale or other changes in operations. Image advertising for a new product is a classic example of a sunk cost, as is an option or investment in assets whose value is specific to a particular situation. Sunk costs reflect commitment, or irreversibility, and are not a part of incremental analysis.

INTERNAL RATE OF RETURN

The **internal rate of return (IRR)** analysis method uses a two-step process involving present value concepts to compute the rate of return from the net cash flows expected from an investment.

1. Calculate the appropriate factor = investment / net annual cash inflow
2. Locate the return in the present value annuity table at the intersection of the factor and the life of the project.

The higher the IRR, the more attractive the project. To make decisions based upon IRR for for mutually exclusive projects, one should compute (IRR – hurdle rate) for each project, rank them from highest to lowest, and accept the highest-ranking project, assuming the computation of (IRR – hurdle rate) > 0.

Advantages of IRR are that it considers all cash flows, considers the time value of money, and helps to compare the hurdle rate.

Disadvantages of IRR are that it does not show dollar improvement in the the value of the firm if the project is accepted, it can be affected by the scale of the project, and there is a possible existence of multiple IRRs.

STATED INTEREST RATES AND EFFECTIVE INTEREST RATES

To make decisions to determine the best loan option or the best investment option, interest rates must be considered. To compare interest rates, one must examine the **stated interest rate**, the rate that the lender will assess per the contract, and the **annual effective interest rate**, the rate that the lender actually receives.

The difference in these two rates is due to the fact that interest will typically be compounded on a more frequent basis than annually, such as monthly or daily. To determine the annual effective interest rate from the stated interest rate, the following computation is done:

Annual effective interest rate = $[1 + (i / f]^f - 1]$, where i = stated interest rate and f = frequency that interest is compounded

PAYBACK METHOD

The **payback method** determines the length of time it takes to recover an initial investment. This amount of time is called the **payback period**. A particular amount of time is selected as a cutoff payback period for the project to pay back the initial investment. The easiest way to think of the payback period is the length of time it takes to break even from an accounting perspective.

The decision Rule for the payback method is that if payback is within an acceptable time limit, one should accept the project.

Advantages of payback method include the following:

- It is very easy to calculate, but it can lead to a wrong decision,
- It puts more emphasis on a quick return of the invested funds, so they may be put to use in other places or in meeting other needs.
- It is easy to apply and simple to understand.

Problems with the payback method include the following:

- It does not consider post-payback cash flows.
- It does not consider the time value of money.
- It does not explicitly consider risk.
- The "acceptable" time period is arbitrary.

Inflation

Inflation is the overall general upward price movement of goods and services. Over time, as the cost of goods and services increase, the value of a dollar falls, because that dollar will not purchase as much as it did previously. Economists think of inflation as a sustained rise in the price of all goods in an economy.

While economists differ in opinion about the root cause of inflation, a factor may be an increase in the amount of currency in circulation, resulting in a fall in its value and a rise in prices.

In the US, the Consumer Price Index (CPI) is one measure of inflation. The CPI is published monthly by the Bureau of Labor Statistics and produces data on changes in the prices paid by urban consumers for a representative basket of goods and services.

Basics of Determining the Cost of Equity and Debt

The **capital asset pricing model** (CAPM) can be used to estimate the cost of equity:

$$E(R_i) = R_f + \beta_i(E(R_m) - R_f)$$

$E(R_i)$ = expected return on capital asset

R_f = risk-free rate

β_i = beta (sensitivity of the asset return to changes in the market return)

$E(R_m)$ = expected return of market

Another method of determining the cost of common equity involves using the constant growth formula.

$$P_0 = D_1 / (K_s - G)$$

P_0 = price of stock

D_1 = anticipated upcoming dividend ($D_1 = D_0 * (1+G)$)

K_s = rate of return

G = anticipated growth rate

The **cost of debt** is equals the current interest cost to borrow new funds. Current interest rates are determined from the present rate available in the financial markets. The financial markets adjust fixed debt interest rates to the present rate through setting debt prices at a discount (current rate > face rate) or premium (current rate < face rate).

Debt Terms

Notes, Registered Bond, Restrictive Covenant, Sinking Fund Provision, Subordinated Debt, Yield to Maturity, and Zero Coupon Bond

Notes: typically denote unsecured debt with maturities shorter than maturities of debentures

Registered bond: bonds for which the bond-issuing company maintains records of bondholders and repays directly to the bondholder

Restrictive covenant: bondholder limits that may pertain to dividends, leasing, and debt ratios

Sinking fund provision: provides for a bond issue's orderly retirement

Subordinated debt: if a company defaults, holders of subordinated debt must give preference to other designated creditors who must be paid first.

Yield to maturity: rate of return resulting from making a bond purchase and holding the bond until its maturity date

Zero coupon bond: at maturity, only pays the face value

Bonds, Call Provision, Collateral Trust Bond, Convertible Bond, Coupon Bond, Debentures, Eurobond, Face Value, and Floating-Rate Bond

Bonds**:** typically secured by a corporate property mortgage

Call provision: feature of bonds that grants the right to buy back all or part of the bond issue for redemption prior to the bond's stated maturity

Collateral trust bond: issued bonds that are secured by a company's financial assets

Convertible bond: can be converted into common stock shares, at the bondholder's discretion, for a fixed price

Coupon bond: makes regular coupon payments; computed by multiplying the coupon rate by the face value

Debentures: unsecured corporate debt

Eurobond: bonds sold in several international bond markets in one primary currency

Face value: maturity date repayment amount

Floating-rate bond: bond that pays interest rates that are periodically adjusted to follow market interest rates

Leverage

Operating Leverage and Financial Leverage

Leverage refers to the use of borrowed funds to earn an overall return higher than the cost of the funds.

Financial leverage is associated with a company's use of debt financing. If a company is experiencing low profits, the company may opt to put off dividend payments. Dividends are the primary cost of equity financing. The primary cost of debt financing is interest; interest must always be paid in a timely manner to keep a company afloat financially.

A company's financial leverage can be computed with the following formula:

% change in earnings per share / % change in earnings before income taxes (EBIT)

Operating leverage is associated with fixed costs as a ratio to the value of the project and is used as an indication of how sensitive net income is to a change in sales.

Operating leverage is calculated by the following formula:

% change in operating income / % change in production volume

Private Debt and Public Debt

Private debt is often issued by smaller firms. There are fewer registration requirements for private debt than for public debt. It is less expensive for companies to issue private debt than to issue public debt.

Public debt is often issued by larger firms. Public debt is more expensive for companies to issue than private debt. Additionally, public debt must be registered with the SEC.

Basics of Long-Term Debt

Foreign Bond, Income Bond, Junk Bond, and Mortgage Bond

For **long-term debt,** interest expenses are tax-deductible to corporate taxpayers. Creditors owning outstanding debt consider it a liability of the company. While creditors generally do not have voting rights, if the company fails to make the necessary payments, the creditors can legally acquire the company's assets to fulfill the debt.

The bond indenture usually lists the amount of issue, the date of issue, the date of maturity, the denomination (par value), the annual coupon, the dates of coupon payments, security, sinking funds, call provisions, and covenants. Bond features that fluctuate over time include the rating, market price, and yield-to-maturity.

Foreign bond are bonds issued by foreign corporations or foreign governments.

Income bonds are bonds that pay interest under the condition that the interest is actually earned.

Junk bond are high-yield bonds issued at high risk for the purchaser to fund leveraged buyouts, mergers, and companies with financial difficulties.

Mortgage bonds are bonds where a company commits particular assets as bond security.

Capital Leases, Operating Leases, and Sale-Leasebacks

A **capital lease** is a method of financing available to companies. Capital leases are typically long-term and cover the asset's useful life. To qualify as a capital lease, at least one of the following criteria must be met:

1. The leased property ownership goes to the lessee at the end of a capital lease.
2. The lease term lasts at least 75% of the lease property's useful life.
3. The minimum lease payment's present value is equal to at least 90% of the lease property's fair value at the beginning of the lease.
4. The lease has a bargain purchase option available at the end of the lease.

An **operating lease** is implemented for the short term; it can be canceled by the lessee. Operating leases are leases that do not qualify to be capital leases and are considered to be rental agreements.

A **sale-leaseback** occurs when, in an effort to raise cash, a company will sell an asset owned by the company and lease it back.

TYPES OF EQUITY

The primary types of equity are common stock and preferred stock. Shareholders are the owners of the company. They buy shares of stock, which represent ownership. Common stock has several advantages. Common stock can provide income, it provides good marketability, and there can be tax-advantages for long-term purchases of common stock. Information required for purchase decisions is readily available to the investor. Common stock can provide a higher-than-average return with proper selection. For long-term accumulation objectives, dividends can be re-invested in additional shares of stock, thereby increasing long term return.

Common stock has several disadvantages. There is no guarantee of return, either through dividends or capital gain. The complete investment is subject to risk of principal loss. The timing of purchases and sales will significantly affect investment return.

BASICS OF ASSET AND INVESTMENT MANGAGEMENT

Asset management is a broad category referring to the monitoring and maintenance of some asset or group of assets, applying not only to tangible assets (e.g. inventory, land, buildings) but to intangible assets (e.g. intellectual property). Its goal is to maximize the cost-effectiveness of operating improving, and disposing of various assets.

Investment management is also a broad category, referring to the monitoring and maintenance of all investments – whether in debt securities, equity securities, or assets – to meet some particular goals as specified by the investors.

TYPES OF MARKETABLE SECURITIES

Types of marketable securities:

1. US Treasury securities, such as T-bills, treasury notes, and treasury bonds, are short-term investments available to companies with the use of repurchase agreements.
2. US federal agency securities are backed by the US government but give slightly higher rates than US Treasury securities.
3. Negotiable certificates of deposit (CDs) are time deposits issued by commercial banks that can be sold to a third party.
4. Short-term tax-exempt municipal securities are short-term investments issued by state and local governments that are generally exempt from federal tax.
5. Bankers' acceptances are drafts that a commercial bank has "accepted."
6. Commercial paper is corporation-issued unsecured promissory notes.
7. Preferred stock and money market preferred stock pays dividends that qualify for the dividends-received deduction.

WORKING CAPITAL MANAGEMENT

Working capital management is the managing of a firm's current assets and current liabilities. Working capital management consists of choosing the levels of cash, marketable securities, receivables, and inventories, as well as the level and mix of types of short-term financing. Working capital management includes the following business relationships:

Sales impact - Granting easy credit and keeping high inventories may help boost sales and fill orders quickly, but these practices also raise costs.

Liquidity - A firm must choose its levels of cash and marketable securities, taking into account needed liquidity and any required compensating balances.

Short-term financing mix – A firm must choose its mix of types of short-term financing, as well as its proportions of short- and long-term financing.

Relations with stakeholders are important to monitor, since suppliers and customers are intimately affected by the management of working capital.

Optimal Capital Structure

Optimal capital structure is the perfect mix of debt and equity to maximize a business's value or to minimize capital costs.

The **weighted-average cost of capital** (WACC) is a firm's overall cost of capital, and it must reflect the required return on the firm's total assets. If a company uses both debt and equity financing, the cost of capital must include the cost of each, weighted to the proportion of each (debt and equity) in the capital structure of the company. WACC weights the cost of equity and the cost of debt by the percentage of each used in a firm's capital structure.

The after-tax rate must be considered because interest on corporate debt is deductible. WACC should be calculated with market values and not book values of debt or equity. WACC will reflect what a firm needs to earn on a new investment; however, the new investment should also reflect a risk level similar to the company's beta used to calculate the firm's return on equity.

Types of Short-Term Financing

Trade Creditors, Factoring, Commercial Bank Lending, and Commercial Paper

1. **Trade creditors** are suppliers to whom a business owes money for raw materials or other components of a product. Businesses are permitted to buy goods or services on credit for the short-term without incurring interest expense. Businesses are often given the option of paying within a designated time period for a discount on purchases.
2. **Factoring** involves raising funds on the security of the company's debts, so that cash is received earlier than if the company waited for the debtors to pay. Most factoring companies offer three services: sales ledger accounting, credit management, and the provision of finance.
3. **Commercial bank lending** operates as a short-term financing source. Commercial banks also provide intermediate-term financing (with maturity between one and ten years). Short-term unsecured bank loans take one of three basic forms: a specific transaction loan, a line of credit, or a revolving credit.
4. **Commercial paper** consists of corporation-issued unsecured promissory notes.

Long-Term Financing

Long-term financing refers to financing that a person or company needs over a longer period of time, usually over one year. It might be used to fund expansion projects for a business (in which case the sources of the financing can be quite complex and enormous); such businesses might seek venture capital as a means of long-term financing. Alternatively, long-term financing might be used to fund a student's tuition at an institution of higher education.

Asset Effectiveness and Efficiency

An asset's **effectiveness** refers to its ability to accomplish the objective for which it is designed, whereas its **efficiency** refers to its ability to accomplish an objective with minimal cost, time, or effort. One goal of asset management is to ensure that assets are being appropriately effective and efficient and to understand how much money should be funneled to pay for the increasing of various assets' effectiveness or efficiency.

Financial Valuations

Fair Value and Fair Market Value

Financial valuation refers to the estimation of the worth (value) of something, whether it is an asset, liability, or equity. Valuations can be needed for many reasons, such as for tax purposes, litigation, or investment analysis.

Two main methods of financial valuation are fair market value and fair value.

Fair market value is, according to IRS Revenue Ruling 59-60, the price to which a willing buyer and willing seller would agree if neither act under compulsion and if both have reasonable knowledge of the relevant facts.

Fair value is, according to ASC 820, the price a seller would receive or a buyer would pay for the transfer of an asset or liability in an orderly transaction between market participants at the date of measurement.

Net Present Value Method

The **net present value method** (NPV) is the method of evaluating a project that recognizes that a dollar received immediately is preferable to a dollar received at some future date. It discounts the cash flow to take into account the time value of money.

The approach is to find the present value of expected net cash flows of an investment, discounted at cost of capital, and subtract from it the initial cash outlay of the project. If the present value is positive, the project will be accepted; if negative, it should be rejected. If the projects under consideration are mutually exclusive, the one with the highest net present value should be chosen. The NPV's problematic features are that it is difficult to explain to non-finance people and that it offers a solution in dollars, not in percentage rates of return.

Internal Rate of Return (IRR) and Net Present Value (NPV)

1. When the IRR = the firm's hurdle rate, NPV = 0
2. When the IRR < the firm's hurdle rate, NPV < 0
3. When the IRR > the firm's hurdle rate, NPV > 0

An accept/reject conflict occurs when NPV says "accept" and IRR says "reject" or NPV says "reject" and IRR says "accept." When projects are independent, no accept/reject conflict will arise. A ranking conflict occurs when one project has a higher NPV than another while the lower NPV project has a higher IRR. Ranking conflicts are unusual but can occur.

These conflicts are relevant only when there are multiple acceptable mutually exclusive projects. Ranking conflicts arise because of:

1. Timing differences in incremental cash flows
2. Magnitude differences in incremental cash flows.

When a conflict arises among mutually exclusive projects, pick the one with the highest NPV.

Some Assumptions Used in Financial Valuations

Because financial valuation is somewhat of an art as well as a science, it is important to remember some important assumptions used when making such valuations.

For instance, when valuing an asset, there can be a number of different purposes and circumstances that would affect the valuation, such as whether its valuation is for financial reporting, a merger, or tax purposes. These considerations can lead to differences in the choice of method or in the interpretation of data within a given method.

Moreover, all valuation models and methods have a limited range of application, and so might call for special judgments in complex circumstances. This includes not only the output of a given model or a method, but the manner by which such information is inputted in the first place.

Financial Transaction Process Controls

Financial transaction process controls are regular procedures designed to prevent or detect errors, fraud, or other failures to comply with established company with a financial transaction process. They can be done in a purely automated fashion, or they can also involve a human to manually oversee various controls. These can consist of reviews or approvals for transactions when the transactions are first initiated, reviews of transactions after they have incurred, and a balance analysis to find oddities in the accounting ledger.

Information Systems and Communications

Basics of Organizational Needs Assessment

Organizational needs assessment is a systematic and methodical process whereby an entity can identify its needs as distinct from its wants. This includes assessing the precise gaps that exist between conditions as they are and conditions as they are desired to be. Roger Kaufman is considered the father of needs assessment (which is broader than organizational needs assessment), having constructed a model which identifies needs and defines them as a gap in results.

Data Capture

Data capture is the immediate and singular obtaining of data when processing transactions. Since cutting costs on small processes is very important—for savings vastly accumulate as the processes are used repetitively—the costs saved through data capture are a feature of the most efficient companies. Oftentimes these companies will immediately acquire data when a transaction occurs, thus simultaneously eliminating the need to re-enter such data (which also brings with it the risk of erroneous re-entry) and making it immediately available for others to utilize.

Computer Processing

Location Perspective, Including Decentralized, Centralized and Distributed

Decentralized processing occurs when the information and processing are maintained on computers at various locations. Typically, the various computers are not connected to a network, so information cannot be shared between computers.

Centralized processing is when all information processing occurs at one designated location. In the past, all information was submitted at various terminals and processed on one mainframe computer. However, it varies now as to how much information is processed by computers that are decentralized versus information that is processed by one centralized computer.

Distributed processing typically will occur in either a batch method or an online real-time method. Various transactions are processed at different sites for one main database. The main database is updated according to the processing of the various transactions.

Computer Systems

Computer systems can be used in businesses for transaction processing or assisting management in decision making. The term "computers" includes supercomputers, mainframe computers, minicomputers, microcomputers, and handheld computers. Computers can vary significantly in size and capabilities. Computer information can be either digital or analog. Digital computers use numerical digits and are computers are typically used in accounting information systems. Analog computers use variable quantity information and are typically used in research and development projects. Computers are composed of hardware and software. Hardware includes the CPU (central processing unit), devices used for input (such as online entry or keying data), devices used for output (such as monitors and printers), and secondary storage components (such as compact disks or floppy disks).

Computer hardware is managed by computer software. Software is made up of both application software (such as spreadsheets and word processing) and systems software (such as operating systems like Windows).

CONTROL ENVIRONMENT AND INFORMATION SYSTEMS IMPACT

Information systems have a significant influence on the control environment. Information systems are involved in both data processing and systems development. **Systems development** will include analyzing systems, programming systems, managing the database, and programming applications. **Data processing** will include controlling data, handling operations, preparing data, and maintaining the data library. A company's choice of using either a mainframe computer or small computers will also influence computerized accounting systems from an **information and communication** standpoint. The necessary computer skills must be maintained for personnel to properly **monitor** a computerized information system and ensure that functions are operating properly.

SYSTEMS DESIGN

Systems design is an important planning process geared towards the mapping out of an information system to achieve a company's objectives. It has a more general element to it, where alternative approaches to the system's design are excluded and the best alternative is selected. The more specific element of systems design involves laying out the selected alternative in greater detail.

ELECTRONIC COMMERCE ENVIRONMENT

ENCRYPTION AND DECRYPTION

The **electronic commerce environment** has vast amounts of multimedia data and distributed, autonomous, and heterogeneous information sources, and it helps to support decision making. It utilizes the internet as an infrastructure. Electronic commerce involves various business activities, such as online marketing, order processing, payment, delivery (information goods) or delivery management, and technical support/customer care. Security and encryption are vital at all levels of electronic commerce.

Encryption is encoding a message into cipher text so that it cannot be easily understood.

Decryption is the opposite – converting the coded message so it can be easily understood.

CONTROL OBJECTIVES FOR INFORMATION AND RELATED TECHNOLOGY (COBIT)

Control Objectives for Information and Related Technology (COBIT) were developed to aid management in fulfilling Section 404 of the Sarbanes-Oxley Act, which requires their oversight of the company's internal controls. COBIT serves as a generally accepted standard for information technology to provide security and control, helping management to apprehend the risks pertinent to information technology. There are three primary objectives to this information technology governance: to ensure that information systems are effective for fulfilling the company's goals, to optimize investments in information technology, and to manage risks and opportunities related to information technology.

COBIT was developed by the IT Governance Institute.

APPLICATION CONTROLS

Application controls relate to specific applications (e.g. revenue, payroll, expenditure) and consist of programmed controls and related manual follow-up procedures.

Application control examples include the following:

1. Batch control totals – establish the accuracy of processing
2. Self-checking digit – a check number is created from the original number and becomes part of the number itself
3. Programmed edit checks – checks written into application programs to reject incomplete, inaccurate, or unreasonable data during the input stage. These edit checks prevent the user from progressing further until resolved.
4. Limit and reasonableness tests – logical tests performed during processing to verify the contents and relationships of records. These errors show up on exception (error) reports.
5. Computer-generated log of input errors
6. Footing and crossfooting

Computer Data Terms

Alphanumeric, Bit, Byte, Character, Field, File, and Record

Computer Data Terms

Alphanumeric – characters that are letters of the alphabet, numbers, or special characters

Bit – smallest unit of computer storage; a binary digit of 0 or 1

Byte – collection of adjoining bits (typically 8) that the computer deals with as a single unit

Character – a symbol, such as a number or letter

Field – collection of linked characters

File – collection of records that are associated with one another and organized in order

Record – fields that are associated rationally in order

General Controls and Operating Controls

General controls pertain to the overall electronic data processing (EDP) environment and corresponding applications, operations controls, changes to existing systems and programs. access to programs, data, equipment, and the development of new programs and systems. A weakness in general controls will have a pervasive effect and make it nearly impossible to rely on specific applications controls. Good general controls ensure that application procedures operate effectively.

Operations controls are implemented to be certain that application programs are correctly used and that the proper data files are used during processing.

Changes to existing programs and systems include controls intended to ensure that modifications to application programs are suitably approved, designed, tested and implemented.

For the **development of new programs and systems**, controls are designed to make sure new application systems are appropriately authorized, designed and tested.

Database and Computer System Networks Controls

Controls are very important in maintaining a database. Controls must be in place for personnel who can access or alter the database. There should be controls in place over the computer terminals and when accessing the database. There should also be controls in place over processing within the database and over classified information. Database users should only be permitted to access or update information for which they are authorized. Since databases are updated throughout each day, there should be a backup and recovery system in place.

Networks are interrelated computers and terminals. Networks can be owned either privately or publicly. For example, a company's network would be privately owned.

Networks may be categorized by the area of network coverage.

Wide area networks (WAN) cover a sizeable geographical region, such as an entire country.

Local area networks (LAN) are privately owned and are located in an area such as a university campus, or even within a single building, such as a business building.

OPERATIONAL EFFECTIVENESS

Operational effectiveness refers to the feature among an organization's practices to maximize the output gained from a particular input, especially to develop new products at a quicker pace and to reduce the defects that may arise.

Since a sizeable part of operational effectiveness is also related to efficiency and automation, information technology plays a large role in boosting a company's operational effectiveness.

INFORMATION TECHNOLOGY

SEGREGATION OF DUTIES

One of the most important areas in the control environment that is impacted by information systems is the **segregation of duties**. It is vitally important to any business to maintain segregation of duties. For example, information systems personnel should not be permitted to authorize financial transactions. Systems development and data processing should be separated to maintain a proper segregation of duties.

AIDS COMPANIES IN IMPLEMENTING COMPANY POLICIES

Since information technology permits many processes to run automatically, it can heavily aid the implementation of company policies by providing greater oversight over company activity (including management, employees, and customers), thus providing all with an additional motive to steer clear of wrongdoing and of innocent error. As with all things, this oversight must have a balance, however; it is easy to lower morale by being overbearing in surveillance.

BREACHES OF SECURITY

While one of the benefits of information technology is the automation which drives it, thus eliminating the need for a human mind to intentionally monitor it, a risk is that the automation's security can be breached by those with sufficient knowledge of the system. This includes **hackers**, who intentionally intrude into information systems to violate laws, obtain informations, or otherwise utilize the system inappropriately. (Sometimes "hackers" are seen as enthusiasts of computers in general, while the term "crackers" – criminal hackers – is used of those who engage in unlawful activities.)

Hackers can have many tools at their disposal, such as **demon dialers**, which will rapidly dial through phone numbers to find modems and then issue a series of usernames and password combinations until it breaks into the system. **Port scanners** will scan a network and its devices in search of various services that are available and unsecured. **Scripts** will search through machines to find any accounts on the machine and whether password attempts to access the machine are limited. If the machine is vulnerable, a **sniffer** will identify and report all usernames and passwords it can find. **Trojan horses** are apparently good programs which operate unexpectedly (and usually harmfully) one the computer's user permits the program to run, and **viruses** are programs that self-duplicate and affix themselves to other programs, doing any amount of damage that it is programmed to do.

Steps Taken to Increase Security

There are various steps one can take to increase the security of one's information technology. **Digital signatures** can help to establish secure website connections and to ensure the validity (though not necessarily the privacy) of any files which are transferred. **Encryption** is a process which encodes data to make it unreadable to anyone who receives the information but lacks the necessary codes or tools for decryption. Encryption can be **symmetric** or **asymmetric**, depending upon whether the key used to encode the unencrypted data and the key needed to decode the encrypted data are the same. In addition to encrypted data, passwords, especially passwords with an unusual use of capital letters and special characters, are clearly helpful in increasing IT security. The number of permitted password attempts should be limited, in order to stave off codes which would rapidly input a number of random password attempts.

Implications the Internet Has on Business

The internet has utterly revolutionized business practices today, leading to the creation of e-commerce, where markets are no longer limited geographically; a typical mom-and-pop shop can now service customers across the world. The internet gives an opportunity for employees to work from a distance (e.g. at home or on vacation), for consumers to become educated about their consumer choices through the vast array of information available, and for retailers (like Amazon) to amass products into single sites and help consumers simplify their shopping process.

Electronic Commerce

Electronic commerce is the buying, selling, marketing, and servicing of products and/or services over computer networks.

Businesses develop methodologies and systems that support:

1. the creation of information sources;
2. effective and efficient interactions among sellers, consumers, intermediaries and producers; and
3. the movement of information across global networks.

Information systems using electronic commerce have risks, including availability, security and confidentiality, online privacy, and processing integrity.

Electronic commerce attempts to increase the speed and efficiency of business transactions and processes and to improve customer relationships and services.

Electronic Funds Transfers and Electronic Data Interchange

Electronic commerce typically involves **electronic funds transfers**, which are electronic monetary payments between businesses or people. Traditional commerce payments involve cash, check or credit cards, whereas electronic cash disbursements can be handled by software wallets, smart cards, electronic cash or debit/credit cards, assuming a business-to-customer model. Business-to-business transactions frequently employ extranets, which are internal, private computer networks that allow controlled access from the outside for specific purposes. Businesses may rely upon **electronic data interchange** (EDI), which is a computer network that facilitates computer-to-computer exchange of electronic documents such as purchase orders, advance shipment notices, and invoices without human intervention or human-readable documents.

Business Process Reengineering (BPR)

Business process reengineering (BPR) is the analysis and subsequent reworking of various workflows and other processes within an organization, with "processes" being understood as sets of related tasks working in conjunction to achieve some particular objective. BPR works to eliminate processes which are not value-adding and to improve processes that add value but inefficiently. Much of BPR can involve the automation of existing processes through the introduction of information technology.

Evolution of the Internet

Changes Business Operations and Organization Cultures

The internet's inception changed business operations by removing the need of a company to appeal only to its local customer base; electronic commerce permitted companies to advertise to geographically distant customers as well. In addition to this, the business's communication with its own employees (in addition to customers) has been steadily improving as the internet has evolved. E-mail, instant messaging, and even teleconferences have drastically changed the means of communication among people in the business world. The business culture is altered not only by this change in communication but by the change in the workers' new ability to work away from the office.

Cloud-Based Systems

Cloud-based systems consist of software and applications whose content and resources are stored not in local computers or servers, but on the internet.

As numerous companies can lease storage space from the same cloud vendor, this arrangement allows for major benefits in terms of economies of scale, reducing the overhead costs of the participating companies. Cloud-based systems also permit employees to work from many different locations, which can be valuable as a backup plan in case of disaster and for employees who would need to telecommute.

Types of Information Systems and Technology Risks

There are a number of information systems available for a company to use. Some types of information systems include data warehouses, enterprise resource planning, enterprise systems, expert systems, geographic information systems, global information systems, and office automation.

-Since information technology is used across organizations as a whole and provide connections for all of their data (rather than simply applying to a few particular processes), there are high risks associated with information technology, should security be breached.

Inventory Management

Enterprise Resources Planning and Material Requirements Planning

Inventory management attempts to make sure there is sufficient inventory to sustain operations. Proper inventory management also looks for ways to decrease costs associated with inventory. Inventory management is concerned with the number of units to order and the timing of orders.

Enterprise resource planning (ERP) is a software solution that addresses the enterprise's needs, taking the process view of the organization, to meet the organizational goals by tightly integrating all functions of an enterprise. ERP plays a major role in inventory management. Firms using ERP can become connected electronically to suppliers.

Material requirements planning is an information system in which sales are converted directly into loads on the facility by subunit and time period. Materials are scheduled more closely, reducing inventories and making delivery times shorter and more predictable. MRP's primary weakness is that MRP is a "push through" system; upon completion of the master schedule, the related goods are pushed through into the process of production, whether they are needed or not.

General Controls

Access Controls to Program and Data and Disaster Recovery

Access controls to program and data are intended to prevent or detect unauthorized changes to programs and files. Access is controlled both through restrictive physical controls and software controls, which limit a) programmer access to production programs, live data files, and job control language; b) operator access to source code and individual elements of data files; and c) user access to defined programs and data files.

All businesses need a **disaster recovery** plan to enable the business to minimize loss in case of a disaster. Firms should plan an alternative way to process business information in case of a disaster and formulate a plan to help continue normal business as soon as possible. All employees should receive training for dealing with disaster situations.

Some Disaster Recovery Steps

A good first step a company can take for disaster recovery is to ensure that it has sufficient backup data. It would be the bare minimum for a company to have some kind of off-site backup. In addition, the company should possess sufficient hardware to run the data software files in case of a disaster.

Additionally, the company should have plans of action in the case of disaster, including decisions to purchase new computers or to have alternate locations where employees can work. These can include "hot sites," where functioning equipment and systems are available to be run with minimal preparation or installation time, and "cold sites," where equipment and power are available but require significant work in preparation to resume the business's operations.

A company's disaster recovery plan also ought to include an outline for how key personnel and certain important stakeholders will be informed, especially for those who would need to make key decisions. There should be a plan for recovery management as well.

Lastly, a company should consider testing different scenarios of disasters in order to better prepare plans for recovery.

Strategic Planning

Market and Risk Analysis

Market analysis is the study of the changes in a particular market as they affect a business's operations. It is part of a larger industry analysis and helps to determine opportunities and threats for a company as part of its SWOT analysis. Companies use market analyses to formulate business strategies in response that aim to capitalize on these opportunities and avert these threats.

Risk analysis is a systematic process of discerning factors which may limit or eliminate the success of some strategy. Risk analysis is valuable to companies who are wishing to improve their strategies by adding elements which serve to prevent or mitigate the effects of future negative events.

Basics of Strategy Development

Implementation, and Monitoring

Strategy development involves the formulation of objectives and designed courses of action, including long-term courses of action, to achieve those objectives. The objectives are generally articulated in relation to the strengths, weaknesses, opportunities, and threats of a business, and they ought to be quantifiable with deadlines. This includes a focus on all the major issues of the strategy, such as the feasibility of the objectives, the resources and time available, the effort that is worth the cost, and so on. An appropriate plan of strategy development also seeks to outline a plan for the strategy's **implementation** and **monitoring**, to ensure constantly or periodically that the steps and levels of the plan are being executed as they ought, with proper changes being made accordingly.

Significance of a Company's Mission and Objectives

The **mission** of a company is the purpose for the company's very existence. It can generally be captured in a mission statement, articulating how the company differs from others and defining the extent of the company's products and customer base. A mission statement sometimes includes what the company seeks to become in the future; if this statement is separate, it can be called a "vision statement." Mission statements and vision statements can be as broad or as narrow as needed.

Objectives provide a specified quantity and deadline as part of the company's strategy. Because of the quantifiable nature of objectives, they are sometimes distinguishes from **goals**, which are broader or unquantified statements of a company's pursuits.

Hierarchy of Strategies

Since company strategies can have multiple dimensions, it is appropriate to speak of the components of a strategy as comprising a **hierarchy of strategies**. This includes three main categories of strategies: a corporate strategy, a business strategy, and a functional strategy.

A **corporate strategy** seeks to cover concerns which address the company as a whole.

A **business strategy** deals with how a company should interact with other businesses in the same industry, including different manners of competition (e.g. focusing on price rather than quality).

A **functional strategy** aims to identify, create, and cultivate a company's competitive advantages.

Corporate Strategy

Two of the Five Strategies: Growth Strategies and Stability Strategies

Growth strategies refer to a company's plan to further develop their products, including concentration (focusing on fewer product lines, cultivating those) and diversification (multipling and developing other product lines). This also involves how companies can collaborate with other companies in the formation and promotion of products (called "synergy").

Stability strategies can be divided into three types: "pause/proceed with caution," which aims to move cautiously until some problem is resolved; "no change," which is the continuation of operations as usual, given the lack of apparent opportunities or threats (this option is usually tacit, not explicitly articulated); and "profit," which involves the reduction of short-term expenditures to stabilize profitability in a time of lower-than-usual sales.

Three of the Five Strategies: Retrenchment Strategies, Portfolio Strategies, and Parenting Strategies

Retrenchment strategies seek to stabilize a business by reducing its size or diversity and cutting expenses. This might involve focusing on particular products or markets, although more extreme retrenchment strategies might involve exiting an industry altogether.

Portfolio strategies involve the company assessing its multiple product lines as if they were components of an investment portfolio. Different products in different stages of their life cycles carry with themselves different levels of risk and expected return, and the company should seek to balance these accordingly, maximizing the expected return and minimizing risk.

Parenting strategies focus on integrating various businesses within the same corporation, distributing resources in a way that maximizes efficiency and effectiveness and taking advantage of economies of scale.

Two Strategies Contained in the Business Strategy

Competitive Strategies and Cooperative Strategies

Competitive strategies pursue the development of a company's competitive advantages. This can be done in different ways: the firm can focus on a **cost leadership strategy**, seeking to be more efficient and cost-reducing than their competitors in a broad market; the firm can focus on **differentiation**, providing different and superior products within a broad market; the firm can have a **cost focus**, having lower costs than competitors in a narrow market; and it can have a **differentiation focus**, pursuing superior products within a narrow market.

Cooperative strategies can be either collusive (which is illegal in many countries, including the USA) or strategic. Strategic cooperative strategies can take a variety of forms, such as mutual service consortia, joint ventures, licensing arrangements, or value-chain partnerships. These alliances will sometimes be formed to combine technological or manufacturing capabilities and to gain access to markets in which the other company has a presence.

Functional Strategy

A **functional strategy** pursues the furthering of a company's competitive advantage through the development of one of its distinctive competencies. A **distinctive competency** is some strength of the company with which the company outperforms competition, which is substantial in the customer's perception of the product's value, and which is transferable for the development of other products. These distinctive competencies can be in the realm of finance, human resources, information technology, logistics, marketing, operating, purchasing, research and development, or other spheres.

Strategy Implementation

Implementation involves developing programs to fulfill business strategies, developing budgets based upon those programs, and developing procedures to execute specific tasks of a program. The implementation of a strategy can have effects on the structure of the entity and on the organizational life cycle.

Strategy Evaluation and Control

Evaluation and control consist of monitoring a strategy as it is executed and pursuing improvements for it, ranging from minor changes in procedure to complete and major changes in mission statement. Proper evaluation and control can include use of a **feedback model**, where performances can be measured and appraised, with corrective action in place for failures to achieve desired performance levels. This can be problematic for performance levels that are difficult to quantify, however.

Strategic Planning

Planning Tools and Techniques

In the process of strategic planning and strategy development, many tools and techniques are available to the management. This can include **market research** to gauge the demands of consumers in different market segments, **cost-benefit analyses** to quantify the pros and cons of various proposed courses of action, **SWOT analyses** to discern the company's strengths, weaknesses, opportunities, and strengths, and **feasibility studies** to identify whether different plans are as attainable or realistic as projected.

Budgets

Zero-Based, Kaizen, and Rolling

A **budget** can be defined as a quantitative allotment of funds for the achievement of some specified objective.

Zero-based budgets are exhaustive and scrutinize every proposed expenditure. These sacrifice efficiency in the short run to maximize it in the long run.

Kaizen budgets include objectives of continuing improvement built-in. An earlier stage of the budget might anticipate so many hours to manufacture some product, while later stages of the budget would anticipate fewer hours to manufacture the same product.

Rolling budgets apply across multiple time periods and are adjusted as each individual time period passes. For instance, a rolling budget might forecast expenditures for a year, but be updated every month to budget for the upcoming twelve months.

Static Budgets, Master Budgets, Capital Budgets, Operating Budgets, and Financial Budgets

Static budgets do not adjust to changes in activity levels.

Master budgets are comprehensive plans encompassing all individual budgets, such as sales, cost of goods sold, capital expenditures and cash, and reflects one activity level. Actual results and original budgeted amounts are compared against one another. Differences between actual and budgeted amounts are called variances. The variances are analyzed to determine the cause and any needed courses of action.

Capital budgets reflect planned expenses for facilities, equipment, new products, and other long-term investments.

Operating budgets include budgets for sales, purchases, cost of goods sold, operating expenses, and the income statement.

Financial budgets include budgets for capital, cash, and the balance sheet.

CAPITAL BUDGETING AND THE ACCOUNTING RATE OF RETURN

Capital budgeting is utilized when evaluating and handling investments that are held for a long-term period. Capital budgeting models include the following:

1. Payback method
2. Net present value
3. Internal rate of return (IRR)
4. Accounting rate of return

Accounting rate of return (ARR) = average net profit / average annual investment

ADVANTAGES OF USING ARR

- Simple to calculate using accounting data
- Earnings of each year are included in calculating the profitability of the project.

DISADVANTAGES OF USING ARR

- Inconsistent with wealth maximization as the objective of the firm
- Includes accruals in calculating "net profit."
- Ignores the time value of money (expected future dollars are erroneously regarded as equal to present dollars).

FLEXIBLE BUDGETS

A **flexible budget** adjusts for varying rates of activity. For example, if sales are higher than originally anticipated, a flexible budget will reflect altered amounts for income and expenses for the varying activity levels.

Management compares actual results, master budgets, and flexible budgets to determine the performance of the organization and to evaluate performance.

Actual amounts may vary from the master budget due to:

1. Sales and other cost-driver activities varying from original anticipated amounts.
2. Revenue or variable costs per unit of activity and fixed costs for the period which were not as anticipated.

FORECASTING

DELPHI TECHNIQUE

Forecasting is an effort to predict future events. Forecasting can be done using either qualitative methods or quantitative methods. Qualitative methods are subjective and rely on management's judgement, opinion, and expertise to develop a prediction for the future. Qualitative methods may include getting opinions from within the organization, such as management or employees. Qualitative methods may include surveys from customers and the Delphi technique.

The **Delphi technique** uses expert opinion to make forecasts through a group consensus. Advantages of the Delphi technique include the following:

1. It is a rapid and efficient way to gain objective information from a group of experts.
2. It involves less effort for a respondent to answer a well-designed questionnaire than to participate in a conference or write a paper.
3. It can be highly motivating for a group of experts to see the responses of knowledgeable persons.
4. The use of systematic procedures applies an air of objectivity to the outcomes.
5. The results of Delphi exercises are subject to greater acceptance on the part of the group.
    1. A disadvantage of the Delphi technique is that each trend is given unilateral consideration on its own merits.

PROBABILITY THEORY

Probability theory helps to provide a quantitative analysis of future uncertainty. It involves the isolation of a **random variable** which has different probabilities of taking different values; and the total set of the possible values which the random variable can take, aligned with the probabilities for each value, is a **probability distribution**. Since it contains all the possible values and their probabilities, the sum of the probabilities for the probability distribution must add up to 1.

By weighting each possible outcome to its corresponding probability and adding each weighted outcome together, one can calculate the **expected value** for some action. For instance, if a given course of action has a 25% chance of $100,000 revenue and a 75% chance of $200,000 revenue, then the expected value for that course of action is $175,000—(25% x $100,000) + (75% x $200,000).

Probability theory also may take into account the **joint probability** of events, that is, the probability that multiple events occur. If two events are independent, their joint probability is the probability of each event taken individually multiplied by one another. If the two events are dependent, then the chance that one event (A) occurs given the occurrence of another event (B)—also denoted as P(A/B)—is different from the event merely that A occurs. To calculate the joint probability for A and B—also denoted as P(AB)—use the following equation:

$$P(AB) = P(A/B) \times P(B) = P(B/A) \times P(A)$$

REGRESSION ANALYSIS, THE COEFFICIENT OF CORRELATION, AND THE COEFFICIENT OF DETERMINATION

Regression analysis seeks to discern a quantifiable relationship between some dependent variable and some independent variable(s), although it does not necessarily establish a causal relationship between or among them. **Simple** regression analysis analyzes a dependent variable in relation to one independent variable, whereas **multiple** regression analysis analyzes a dependent variable in relation to at least two independent variables.

The **coefficient of correlation** (R) calculates the degree to which a dependent variable and a single independent variable are linearly related. A value of 1 or -1 signifies a perfectly linear relationship between the two—i.e. all the (x,y) points for the two variables form a perfectly straight line—whereas a value of 0 signifies that no linear relation at all exists between them; the (x,y) points for the variables would be a pure scatterplot. The values for R must fall between 1 and -1.

The **coefficient of determination** is the square of the coefficient of correlation, and so can also be represented as R^2. It therefore must lie between 0 and 1. The closer R^2 is to 1, the more we can be sure that independent variable is responsible for whatever variability there is with the dependent variable.

INTEGRATED BUSINESS PLANNING (IBP)

Integrated business planning (IBP) seeks to holistically provide a model for a company, interrelating its different functions and organizational segments in order to maximize the use of technology and to link different forms of planning (operational, strategic, and financial planning). IBP helps companies to maximize efficiency and provides them a competitive advantage by explicating the relations among the different facets of the company.

BASICS OF PERFORMANCE MEASURES

Due to the many different facets of an organization's performance, it can be difficult to accurately measure. A company's financial statements can help to show its financial position for a given time or timespan, but **scorecards** can help to better measure non-financial features. Scorecards may require additional judgment and effort to create, since they need to be specifically helpful for a particular industry or company and therefore could mislead a company for which the scorecard is not intended. Moreover, the preparation of scorecards is not a strictly scientific process, but requires judgment which is not standardized or codified.

Balanced scorecards should seek to answer information concerning the business's customers, innovation, strategies, and financial information.

QUALITY CONTROL

Quality control is the process by which all the steps and materials working towards a final product are examined. This can include an analysis of process controls, general knowledge, skills, and competence, and worker morale, in addition to more concrete appraisals of finished goods.

Quality control programs have a number of costs. Some of these costs include prevention costs (the costs to avoid future deficiencies), appraisal costs (the costs of evaluating products for deficiencies), interior failure costs (the costs to fix deficient products before they are shipped), exterior failure costs (the costs to fix deficient products after they are shipped), and opportunity costs (the costs of sales lost due to customer dissatisfaction with a product).

QUALITY MEASURES

There are several different ways in which one can measure quality.

Aesthetics concern the desirability of the product's appearance to the senses.

Conformance concerns the extent to which a product adapts to product standards.

Durability concerns the length of time a customer can expect before the product no longer functions as intended.

Features are non-essential characteristics or functions beyond what is part of a product's ordinary operations.

Perceived quality concerns the general reputation afforded to the product, and is quite important in the absence of more quantifiable measures (or if there already is a parity of such measures with competitors' products).

Performance concerns the product's capability to function as advertised.

Reliability concerns the degree to which a product will require no supplemental maintenance.

Serviceability concerns the easiness of repairing the product, should it need repair.

Implementing Optimal Practices

The difference in costs between the best organizations and the next-best ones is often great, due to an accumulation of savings stemming from a high number of repeated and apparently minor events in various processes for the company. Some of the optimal practices leading to this cost leadership include the following:

- The best companies stress results over tasks and organize their work accordingly.
- Data capture programs are utilized to ensure that accurate data is acquired and immediately available for use elsewhere, thus eliminating the cost of transfer and the chance of errors in data input.
- Automated controls aid a company in (more or less) effortlessly ensuring that data is without error.
- Uses of recent technology can permit a company to have geographically distant locations (thus helping to increase or improve communications with customers) that are nonetheless integrated in communications and data use.
- Online processing permits companies to process almost all of their transactions electronically.

Operations Management

Basics of Performance Management

Impact of Measures on Behavior

Performance management (PM) is a very broad practice which seeks to ensure that objectives are being accomplished effectively and efficiently, and to improve areas where objectives are not being thus accomplished. There are levels of generality to which performance management can apply: to organizations as a whole, to departments, to employees, and to specific processes.

-Measures not only serve to indicate the performance levels of various functions for an organization. They also serve (for the human parts of the business) to affect the behavior. Knowing that one's performance is monitored can help to motivate a person to do better work, although there also can be the negative effect of resentment, if the employee feels that the company's measurements indicate a lack of trust. Consequently, there should be a balance in the amount of monitoring done by a company, and management should be sure to make their intentions clear in doing the measurement in the first place.

Financial and Nonfinancial Measures

Financial measures of performance management consist, as would be expected, of the financial statements relevant to the area being examined. For the company as a whole, the public financial statements can serve to provide financial measures, and other financial information can be acquired to understand the financial impact of different segments of the organization. This can include cash flow, working capital, profit margin, operating margin, and a number of liquidity, profitability, and other ratios.

Nonfinancial measures are more difficult to attain, since they are by nature less quantifiable, even though they have an effect on financial information. This can include such things as employee morale, customer satisfaction, and company reputation.

Impact of Marketing Practices

Marketing practices serve to impact a firm's performance in several ways. One would simply be by disseminating information about the firm's products to consumers, making them aware of whatever competitive advantages the firm has to distinguish itself from competitors, so that consumers can consciously compare them. Another would be to build brand loyalty and to make the consumer associate certain ideas with that particular brand. The more firms do marketing in order to appeal to the market segments where they think their products will flourish, the more performance will improve; and then it is just a matter of avoiding diminishing returns.

Basics of Incentive Compensation

Incentive compensation is the payment of a person not for the time spent doing work but according to the results of work. While it is good to provide an incentive for workers to work harder, it also can have its negative effects. Some workers desire a stable job where they do not see themselves as constantly under pressure to perform or else forfeit significant amounts of payment. On the other hand, some workers are perfectly content to work at a lethargic pace (or to refrain from altogether), in which case incentive compensation could help to keep them honest. In addition, for upper-level workers, such as management and officers, their incentive compensation can sometimes motivate them to artificially improve information, to "cook the books." Hence, for them, it is especially important to have a balance of fixed salary and incentive compensation, depending upon the nature of the work and the person involved.

Basics of Cost Measurement Methods and Techniques

In cost-benefit analyses, a quantitative comparison of costs and benefits is crucial, and this is why there must be particular methods and techniques for cost measurement. For any particular course of action, the cost must be measured in its full effects, including its effects on users and participants, its effects on non-users and non-participants, its externality effects, and its option value and other social benefits.

Manufacturing Cost Elements

Conversion Cost, Prime Cost, Product Costs, and Period Costs

There are three **manufacturing cost elements**: direct materials, direct labor, and manufacturing overhead. **Direct materials** consist of all the materials which compose the final product and can easily be traced to it. **Direct labor** is all the labor used to modify the direct materials into the final product; these costs also should easily be traced to the final product. **Manufacturing overhead** is the remainder of the costs which make a product, and thus consist of all the costs which cannot be easily traced to a product.

Conversion cost is the cost to convert the direct materials to the final product and thus is the sum of direct labor and manufacturing overhead.

Prime cost is the total expense for the materials and labor used in production and thus is the sum of direct labor and direct materials.

Product costs are all the costs which can be attributed to inventory (whether directly or indirectly related to the actual physical products). These become part of the cost of goods sold when the products are sold, and all manufacturing cost elements fall under the heading of product costs.

Period costs are not related to the production process and thus not a part of inventory. Rather than being part of the cost of goods sold, these are expensed according to the time period in which they took place. Examples of period costs would be selling and administrative expenses.

Cost Behavior

Cost behavior can be understood on an aggregate/total basis, or on a unit basis. **Fixed costs**, which remain constant over a given period and range of activity (the "relevant range"), are the same in aggregate and decrease in unit cost for each unit of production. (Fixed costs also decrease *at a decreasing pace*: the second unit produced halves the fixed cost per unit, but the fixed cost is halved again only when 4, 8, 16, etc. units are produced.) **Variable costs**, on the other hand, have a constant price per unit but linearly increase as an aggregate cost as more units are produced. There are also **mixed (semivariable) costs**, which are partly fixed and partly variable.

Some variable costs are **step-variable costs**, for which the total cost is constant over a certain interval but then shifts upward for the next interval. (And thus the graph for step-variable costs looks like a series of steps.) An example of this might be the cost for supervisors for a given number of workers. For 1-10 workers, there might be only one supervisor needed, but the supervisor cost would immediately double if a second supervisor is needed for 11-20 workers.

Cost of Goods Manufactured Schedule

The **cost of goods manufactured schedule** seeks to represent the number of products which were created from direct materials and thus transferred to finished inventory over a given period of time.

There usually will be work already in process at the beginning of the period and at the end of the period, which the schedule takes account of. The following are the equations included in the schedule:

1. Beginning inventory + purchases = materials available for use
2. Materials available for use – ending inventory = direct materials used
3. Indirect materials + indirect labor + miscellaneous = manufacturing overhead
4. Direct materials used + direct labor + manufacturing overhead = total current manufacturing costs incurred
5. Beginning work-in-process + total current manufacturing costs incurred = total manufacturing costs to account for
6. Total manufacturing costs to account for – ending work-in-process = cost of goods manufactured

Cost-Volume-Profit Analysis

Target Net Income and Break-Even Analysis

Cost-Volume-Profit (CVP) analysis reviews fluctuations in all costs, levels of volume, and the final results of these fluctuations on total profits. CVP analysis is usually depicted as either a graph or a formula, and is used to gain an understanding of the relationship between costs, business volume, and profitability.

Target net income is determined by use of the following formula:

Sales = variable costs + fixed costs + target net income

The **break-even point** is the sales level at which operating income is zero (where total revenue = total expenses).

$$\text{Contribution margin (CM)} = \text{sales} - \text{variable costs}$$

$$\text{Contribution margin ratio} = \frac{\text{contribution margin}}{\text{sales}}$$

$$\text{Break} - \text{even point (in units)} = \frac{\text{fixed costs} + \text{operating income}}{\text{CM per unit}}$$

$$\text{Break} - \text{even point (in dollars)} = \frac{\text{fixed costs} + \text{operating income}}{\text{CM ratio}}$$

Relevant Costs

Relevant costs consist of all the future costs which can be expected and which are different among the presented alternatives. It is crucial that only the relevant costs be considered when making a decision, for it is often too easy to include unimportant costs, which can end up hurting the company.

Relevant costs should include **avoidable costs** (costs which would be avoided if some activity is chosen or not), **marginal costs** (the further cost of producing one more unit for a product), **out-of-pocket costs** (very near cash outflows), and **opportunity costs** (the sum benefits which are given up from the next-best alternative that is not selected).

Relevant costs should always exclude **sunk costs**, which are costs that occurred in the past. Sometimes people will be tempted to pursue a course of action since the historical cost of it makes them feel like they now have to make the cost "worth it," but the historical cost should simply be excluded when choices are made among alternatives.

PRODUCT PRICING

Product pricing must incorporate a number of different factors in order to achieve its primary goal of profit-maximization. The goal is to increase prices enough that costs are covered while decreasing them enough that there is enough consumer demand to result in a significant number of purchases. Thus, to gather all this information, one needs data and principles from accounting, marketing, engineering, economics, and statistics.

One can use the **contribution margin approach**, which bases product prices on the variable cost and relevant fixed costs of each additional unit produced.

One can utilize **cost-plus pricing**, which starts with the products cost and then adds a specific markup percentage to arrive at the selling price.

Some companies also employ **predatory pricing**, which is a deliberate attempt to set prices very low to drive out competition and then raise prices once the company has secured a monopoly. Modern antitrust policy forbids predatory pricing.

DIRECT (VARIABLE) COSTING

Direct costing (also called **variable costing**) allocates all direct materials, direct labor, and variable manufacturing overhead costs as product costs and allocates fixed manufacturing overhead costs as period costs. Consequently, all but fixed manufacturing overhead costs are included as costs of inventory, and the income statement starts with sales and subtracts all variable costs to arrive at the company's contribution margin.

Direct costing can be employed only for internal reporting purposes; GAAP requires that absorption costing (where all variable and fixed manufacturing costs are included in inventory) be used for external financial reporting. This is an important difference, for absorption costing and direct costing yield different net incomes depending on the level of production. If the units produced exceed units sold, absorption cost reveals a higher profit than direct costing, and vice versa. Only when units produced and units sold are identical do absorption and direct costing yield the same profit.

PROCESS MANAGEMENT

Process management seeks to monitor, analyze, and improve various particular business processes for the sake of improving efficiency, effectiveness, profitability, and customer satisfaction. This includes the management of both business processes and manufacturing processes, though it is different from program management, which is broader and seeks to also understand and develop the workings of several interrelated processes and projects.

PROCESS COSTING

Process costing seeks to group production costs according to departments or to phases of production. Unit costs are determined by taking the total costs for a particular cost center and dividing them by the units produced, and thus is helpful for organizations which produce a large number of homogeneous products continuously and in a series of processes.

STEPS IN PROCESS COST ACCOUNTING

Steps in **process cost accounting**

Step 1: Summarize the flow of production in physical units.

Step 2: Compute output in terms of equivalent units.

Equivalent units are a measure of the amount of work done during a period expressed in terms of fully complete units of output. (Equivalent units percentage = completed units * process completed.)

Step 3: Summarize the total costs to account for.

Step 4: Compute the cost per equivalent unit.

Step 5: Assign costs to units completed and to units in ending work-in-process.

Spoilage

Spoilage consists of any production which does not result in suitable finished products. Deficient goods can be classed as "spoiled," in which case they are scrapped and sold for salvage value, or "defective," in which case they are sold as such at a discount to the customer if they are not repaired. If defective goods are reworked, the cost is generally charged to manufacturing overhead.

Normal spoilage is an ordinary part of any manufacturing process, is generally avoidable (since all manufacturing is imperfect in some way), and is thus included within the cost of goods sold.

Abnormal spoilage is any spoilage beyond the normal spoilage rate which is estimated and established by the company management, and should be viewed as a controllable loss due to inefficiency. It is not included in cost of goods sold but recorded as a loss.

Any manufacturing process naturally produces **scrap**, which consists of the materials left over from the process that may be sold or reused. (A strength of successful companies is to find novel ways to reuse scrap.) **Waste** cannot be reused, though there is a cost for its removal.

Cost Allocation

The appropriate allocation of costs to inventory or other financial statement categories is an important aspect of the financial reporting process.

One important distinction in this is the difference between joint products and by-products. **Joint products** are two products which are usually both intended to be produced by the same process working on the same direct materials, both products having a significant sales value. **By-products** are usually unintended results of a production process and have a minor sales value. For both of these, there is a **split-off point** at which the separate products become identifiable.

There are three basics methods by which costs can be allocated for joint products. The **relative market (sales) value method** allocates cost according to the sales for each product. The **net realizable value method** allocates costs according to the products' net realizable value, which is the difference between their sales value and the estimated costs to finish and sell the product from the split-off point. The **physical measures method** allocates costs according to some physical feature of the product in relation to the direct materials, such as the product's weight.

For by-products, one can subtract either by-product revenue or the by-products' net realizable value from the main products' cost.

Activity-Based Costing (ABC)

Activity-based costing (ABC) seeks to allocate costs according to activities performed by the organization and subsequently to assign them to particular products based on the products' utilization of such activities. The steps of ABC are to

1. identify discrete, relevant, material activities;
2. organize activities according to cost centers (such as R&D or marketing), which can consist of one or more activities;
3. discern significant elements of indirect costs;
4. specify cost drivers (the unit of an activity causing a change in activity cost) and assign costs to activities and activities to products;
5. make a cost-flow chart;
6. utilize appropriate cost-conversion tools;
7. collect data for the system; and
8. use the cost-flow model to formulate appropriate costing rates.

Steps in Developing an Activity-Based Costing System

Steps in developing an **activity-based costing system**:

Step 1: Identify the activities.

Step 2: Estimate the total indirect costs of each activity.

Step 3: Identify the allocation base for each activity.

Step 4: Estimate the total quantity of each allocation base.

Step 5: Compute the cost allocation rate for each activity.

$$\text{Allocation rate} = \frac{\text{estimated total indirect costs of activity}}{\text{estimated total quantity of cost allocation base}}$$

Step 6: Obtain the actual quantity of each allocation base used by the activity.

Step 7: Allocate the costs.

Allocated activity costs = cost allocation rate * actual quantity of the activity cost allocation base used

Standard Cost Accounting

Standard cost accounting does not allocate the actual costs of direct materials, direct labor, and manufacturing overhead to particular products, but instead assigns an estimated (standard) cost, after which variances between standard costs and actual costs are calculated. The value of using these estimates is that it helps management to identify problems which might be concealed if actual costs were not compared to a standard.

There are a number of different kinds of variances: price variances, efficiency variances, spending variances, total fixed overhead variances, and others.

Some Benefits of Process Management

Process management can lead to a number of distinct benefits. It improves accountability, since processes are constantly monitored to look out for unusual activity. It also improves the reliability of processes, since errors or misuses are easily located and corrected. It helps to simplify conformity with established regulations, since compliance with legal obligations can be tracked on a daily basis rather than all at once. Appropriate management of processes also helps to avoid waste, since the additional costs of various processes can be spotted much more easily. Lastly, process management helps to promote safer work conditions, since physical resources and confidential information can be better protected from error or misuse.

SHARED SERVICES, OUTSOURCING, AND OFFSHORING

Shared services involves the consolidation of services into one part of an organization when it was previously used among many different departments. This helps to reduce costs by centralizing an oft-used operation and thus getting rid of redundancy. It is commonly used today for finance, human resources, and information technology.

Outsourcing refers to the contractual transfer of operations normally done within a business to a different organization, sometimes to firms of foreign nations. The opposite of this, where a company purchases operations for which it previously depended on another firm (i.e. vertical integration), is called **insourcing**.

Offshoring is the moving of a company's operations to a foreign country. This can occur for processes dealing with operation (like manufacturing) or for other processes (like accounting and customer support).

MANAGEMENT CHARACTERISTICS FOR PERFORMANCE IMPROVEMENT

There are a number of characteristics possessed by managers who can lead their organizations to achieve high levels of performance. Good managers are clear in articulating their understandings of their and others' particular roles and responsibilities, thus having an open and comprehensive view of the organization's operations and processes. They also set realistic but motivating (and non-conflicting) short- and long-term objectives and have a consistent and rational decision process which leads to well-formed plans of action with clear schedules and steps.

JUST-IN-TIME PURCHASING AND PRODUCTION SYSTEMS

Just-in-time (JIT) purchasing is the purchase of goods or materials such that a delivery immediately precedes demand or use. Firms who are migrating toward the use of JIT purchasing believe that inventory carrying cost has been significantly underestimated in the past.

JIT production systems assume a "demand pull" approach; goods are only manufactured to satisfy customer orders. A JIT system has a focus on total quality management; firms attempt to decrease manufacturing lead time and setup time. Employees should be multi-skilled and able to handle various duties. A successful JIT system maintains good relationships with suppliers.

JIT systems permit backflush costing, a basic costing system. **Backflush costing** puts off recording some or all of the journal entries pertaining to the cycle from buying direct materials to the finished goods sales. In backflush costing, if journal entries for one or more stages in the cycle are omitted, the journal entries for a subsequent stage use normal or standard costs to work backward to flush out the costs in the cycle for which journal entries were not made.

DEMAND FLOW TECHNOLOGY AND THE THEORY OF CONSTRAINTS

Demand flow technology seeks to arrange business processes and operations to flow in response to customer demand. It involves a number of mathematical tools designed to measure daily customer demand and have business processes function accordingly.

The theory of constraints is based upon the understanding of a chain's being only as strong as its weakest link. It seeks to identify vulnerabilities and weaknesses, viewing those as the ultimate constraints, and improving them.

Six Sigma

Six Sigma is a strategy for business management which pursues to maximize the effectiveness and efficiency of production processes by isolating causes of product defects and removing or repairing them. Six Sigma utilizes a number of statistical methods according to a definite series of steps in order to achieve this. Since a "sigma rating" refers to the infrequency with which a given process produces defective products, "six sigma" refers to a particular level of that, namely, 3.4 defects per million units of output.

Basics of Project Management

Project management refers to the comprehensive practice of organizing, planning, distributing, and guiding various resources (including human resources) to achieve particular objectives, with projects being understood as temporary undertakings with a defined beginning, end, and benchmarks. Projects can be contrasted with the ordinary and repeated operations of a business. Project management seeks to accomplish these projects given the constraints of scope, time, and budgets, and involves the steps of planning, implementation, and monitoring.

Roles of Project Managers and Project Members

Project managers have a number of roles for the oversight of their projects. They ought to construct the plan itself and keep track of the project's stakeholders, risk, schedule, budget, and conflicts, in addition to ensuring that each project member is doing his assignment properly and is sufficiently motivated unto that end. These roles might be added to and contextualized according to the specific industry and characteristics of the company.

Project members' roles are less comprehensive and overarching but nonetheless indispensable. They ought to communicate to the manager their progress or obstacles when performing their particular tasks, and they also ought to ensure that their relations with other project members are sufficiently harmonious to evade conflict that would inhibit the project's efficiency and effectiveness.

Steering Committee

A **steering committee** is a higher form of oversight than a project manager, ordinarily composed of high-level stakeholders and experts who can express their desires and plans in an attempt to steer the organization as a whole. Their input can be on a variety of functions, issues, and processes within the organization, including marketing, technology, budgets, resources, company policy, and long-term objectives.

Project Risks

Resource, Scope, Cost, and Deliverables

When managing a project, there are a number of factors to consider in attempting to achieve the project's objectives and reduce the risk that the project will fail to meet some of its goals. This includes appropriate management when it comes to the resources allocated to the completion of the project, the scope of the project (ensuring that it is significant enough but not unrealistic), the cost of the project (especially in relation to the allocated budget), and the quality of deliverables (the outputs which will be transferred to customers).

How to Overcome Test Anxiety

Just the thought of taking a test is enough to make most people a little nervous. A test is an important event that can have a long-term impact on your future, so it's important to take it seriously and it's natural to feel anxious about performing well. But just because anxiety is normal, that doesn't mean that it's helpful in test taking, or that you should simply accept it as part of your life. Anxiety can have a variety of effects. These effects can be mild, like making you feel slightly nervous, or severe, like blocking your ability to focus or remember even a simple detail.

If you experience test anxiety—whether severe or mild—it's important to know how to beat it. To discover this, first you need to understand what causes test anxiety.

Causes of Test Anxiety

While we often think of anxiety as an uncontrollable emotional state, it can actually be caused by simple, practical things. One of the most common causes of test anxiety is that a person does not feel adequately prepared for their test. This feeling can be the result of many different issues such as poor study habits or lack of organization, but the most common culprit is time management. Starting to study too late, failing to organize your study time to cover all of the material, or being distracted while you study will mean that you're not well prepared for the test. This may lead to cramming the night before, which will cause you to be physically and mentally exhausted for the test. Poor time management also contributes to feelings of stress, fear, and hopelessness as you realize you are not well prepared but don't know what to do about it.

Other times, test anxiety is not related to your preparation for the test but comes from unresolved fear. This may be a past failure on a test, or poor performance on tests in general. It may come from comparing yourself to others who seem to be performing better or from the stress of living up to expectations. Anxiety may be driven by fears of the future—how failure on this test would affect your educational and career goals. These fears are often completely irrational, but they can still negatively impact your test performance.

Elements of Test Anxiety

As mentioned earlier, test anxiety is considered to be an emotional state, but it has physical and mental components as well. Sometimes you may not even realize that you are suffering from test anxiety until you notice the physical symptoms. These can include trembling hands, rapid heartbeat, sweating, nausea, and tense muscles. Extreme anxiety may lead to fainting or vomiting. Obviously, any of these symptoms can have a negative impact on testing. It is important to recognize them as soon as they begin to occur so that you can address the problem before it damages your performance.

The mental components of test anxiety include trouble focusing and inability to remember learned information. During a test, your mind is on high alert, which can help you recall information and stay focused for an extended period of time. However, anxiety interferes with your mind's natural processes, causing you to blank out, even on the questions you know well. The strain of testing during anxiety makes it difficult to stay focused, especially on a test that may take several hours. Extreme anxiety can take a huge mental toll, making it difficult not only to recall test information but even to understand the test questions or pull your thoughts together.

Effects of Test Anxiety

Test anxiety is like a disease—if left untreated, it will get progressively worse. Anxiety leads to poor performance, and this reinforces the feelings of fear and failure, which in turn lead to poor performances on subsequent tests. It can grow from a mild nervousness to a crippling condition. If allowed to progress, test anxiety can have a big impact on your schooling, and consequently on your future.

Test anxiety can spread to other parts of your life. Anxiety on tests can become anxiety in any stressful situation, and blanking on a test can turn into panicking in a job situation. But fortunately, you don't have to let anxiety rule your testing and determine your grades. There are a number of relatively simple steps you can take to move past anxiety and function normally on a test and in the rest of life.

Physical Steps for Beating Test Anxiety

While test anxiety is a serious problem, the good news is that it can be overcome. It doesn't have to control your ability to think and remember information. While it may take time, you can begin taking steps today to beat anxiety.

Just as your first hint that you may be struggling with anxiety comes from the physical symptoms, the first step to treating it is also physical. Rest is crucial for having a clear, strong mind. If you are tired, it is much easier to give in to anxiety. But if you establish good sleep habits, your body and mind will be ready to perform optimally, without the strain of exhaustion. Additionally, sleeping well helps you to retain information better, so you're more likely to recall the answers when you see the test questions.

Getting good sleep means more than going to bed on time. It's important to allow your brain time to relax. Take study breaks from time to time so it doesn't get overworked, and don't study right before bed. Take time to rest your mind before trying to rest your body, or you may find it difficult to fall asleep.

Along with sleep, other aspects of physical health are important in preparing for a test. Good nutrition is vital for good brain function. Sugary foods and drinks may give a burst of energy but this burst is followed by a crash, both physically and emotionally. Instead, fuel your body with protein and vitamin-rich foods.

Also, drink plenty of water. Dehydration can lead to headaches and exhaustion, especially if your brain is already under stress from the rigors of the test. Particularly if your test is a long one, drink water during the breaks. And if possible, take an energy-boosting snack to eat between sections.

Along with sleep and diet, a third important part of physical health is exercise. Maintaining a steady workout schedule is helpful, but even taking 5-minute study breaks to walk can help get your blood pumping faster and clear your head. Exercise also releases endorphins, which contribute to a positive feeling and can help combat test anxiety.

When you nurture your physical health, you are also contributing to your mental health. If your body is healthy, your mind is much more likely to be healthy as well. So take time to rest, nourish your body with healthy food and water, and get moving as much as possible. Taking these physical steps will make you stronger and more able to take the mental steps necessary to overcome test anxiety.

Mental Steps for Beating Test Anxiety

Working on the mental side of test anxiety can be more challenging, but as with the physical side, there are clear steps you can take to overcome it. As mentioned earlier, test anxiety often stems from lack of preparation, so the obvious solution is to prepare for the test. Effective studying may be the most important weapon you have for beating test anxiety, but you can and should employ several other mental tools to combat fear.

First, boost your confidence by reminding yourself of past success—tests or projects that you aced. If you're putting as much effort into preparing for this test as you did for those, there's no reason you should expect to fail here. Work hard to prepare; then trust your preparation.

Second, surround yourself with encouraging people. It can be helpful to find a study group, but be sure that the people you're around will encourage a positive attitude. If you spend time with others who are anxious or cynical, this will only contribute to your own anxiety. Look for others who are motivated to study hard from a desire to succeed, not from a fear of failure.

Third, reward yourself. A test is physically and mentally tiring, even without anxiety, and it can be helpful to have something to look forward to. Plan an activity following the test, regardless of the outcome, such as going to a movie or getting ice cream.

When you are taking the test, if you find yourself beginning to feel anxious, remind yourself that you know the material. Visualize successfully completing the test. Then take a few deep, relaxing breaths and return to it. Work through the questions carefully but with confidence, knowing that you are capable of succeeding.

Developing a healthy mental approach to test taking will also aid in other areas of life. Test anxiety affects more than just the actual test—it can be damaging to your mental health and even contribute to depression. It's important to beat test anxiety before it becomes a problem for more than testing.

Study Strategy

Being prepared for the test is necessary to combat anxiety, but what does being prepared look like? You may study for hours on end and still not feel prepared. What you need is a strategy for test prep. The next few pages outline our recommended steps to help you plan out and conquer the challenge of preparation.

Step 1: Scope Out the Test

Learn everything you can about the format (multiple choice, essay, etc.) and what will be on the test. Gather any study materials, course outlines, or sample exams that may be available. Not only will this help you to prepare, but knowing what to expect can help to alleviate test anxiety.

Step 2: Map Out the Material

Look through the textbook or study guide and make note of how many chapters or sections it has. Then divide these over the time you have. For example, if a book has 15 chapters and you have five days to study, you need to cover three chapters each day. Even better, if you have the time, leave an extra day at the end for overall review after you have gone through the material in depth.

If time is limited, you may need to prioritize the material. Look through it and make note of which sections you think you already have a good grasp on, and which need review. While you are studying, skim quickly through the familiar sections and take more time on the challenging parts.

Write out your plan so you don't get lost as you go. Having a written plan also helps you feel more in control of the study, so anxiety is less likely to arise from feeling overwhelmed at the amount to cover.

Step 3: Gather Your Tools

Decide what study method works best for you. Do you prefer to highlight in the book as you study and then go back over the highlighted portions? Or do you type out notes of the important information? Or is it helpful to make flashcards that you can carry with you? Assemble the pens, index cards, highlighters, post-it notes, and any other materials you may need so you won't be distracted by getting up to find things while you study.

If you're having a hard time retaining the information or organizing your notes, experiment with different methods. For example, try color-coding by subject with colored pens, highlighters, or post-it notes. If you learn better by hearing, try recording yourself reading your notes so you can listen while in the car, working out, or simply sitting at your desk. Ask a friend to quiz you from your flashcards, or try teaching someone the material to solidify it in your mind.

Step 4: Create Your Environment

It's important to avoid distractions while you study. This includes both the obvious distractions like visitors and the subtle distractions like an uncomfortable chair (or a too-comfortable couch that makes you want to fall asleep). Set up the best study environment possible: good lighting and a comfortable work area. If background music helps you focus, you may want to turn it on, but otherwise keep the room quiet. If you are using a computer to take notes, be sure you don't have any other windows open, especially applications like social media, games, or anything else that could distract you. Silence your phone and turn off notifications. Be sure to keep water close by so you stay hydrated while you study (but avoid unhealthy drinks and snacks).

Also, take into account the best time of day to study. Are you freshest first thing in the morning? Try to set aside some time then to work through the material. Is your mind clearer in the afternoon or evening? Schedule your study session then. Another method is to study at the same time of day that you will take the test, so that your brain gets used to working on the material at that time and will be ready to focus at test time.

Step 5: Study!

Once you have done all the study preparation, it's time to settle into the actual studying. Sit down, take a few moments to settle your mind so you can focus, and begin to follow your study plan. Don't give in to distractions or let yourself procrastinate. This is your time to prepare so you'll be ready to fearlessly approach the test. Make the most of the time and stay focused.

Of course, you don't want to burn out. If you study too long you may find that you're not retaining the information very well. Take regular study breaks. For example, taking five minutes out of every hour to walk briskly, breathing deeply and swinging your arms, can help your mind stay fresh.

As you get to the end of each chapter or section, it's a good idea to do a quick review. Remind yourself of what you learned and work on any difficult parts. When you feel that you've mastered the material, move on to the next part. At the end of your study session, briefly skim through your notes again.

But while review is helpful, cramming last minute is NOT. If at all possible, work ahead so that you won't need to fit all your study into the last day. Cramming overloads your brain with more information than it can process and retain, and your tired mind may struggle to recall even previously learned information when it is overwhelmed with last-minute study. Also, the urgent nature of cramming and the stress placed on your brain contribute to anxiety. You'll be more likely to go to the test feeling unprepared and having trouble thinking clearly.

So don't cram, and don't stay up late before the test, even just to review your notes at a leisurely pace. Your brain needs rest more than it needs to go over the information again. In fact, plan to finish your studies by noon or early afternoon the day before the test. Give your brain the rest of the day to relax or focus on other things, and get a good night's sleep. Then you will be fresh for the test and better able to recall what you've studied.

Step 6: Take a Practice Test

Many courses offer sample tests, either online or in the study materials. This is an excellent resource to check whether you have mastered the material, as well as to prepare for the test format and environment.

Check the test format ahead of time: the number of questions, the type (multiple choice, free response, etc.), and the time limit. Then create a plan for working through them. For example, if you have 30 minutes to take a 60-question test, your limit is 30 seconds per question. Spend less time on the questions you know well so that you can take more time on the difficult ones.

If you have time to take several practice tests, take the first one open book, with no time limit. Work through the questions at your own pace and make sure you fully understand them. Gradually work up to taking a test under test conditions: sit at a desk with all study materials put away and set a timer. Pace yourself to make sure you finish the test with time to spare and go back to check your answers if you have time.

After each test, check your answers. On the questions you missed, be sure you understand why you missed them. Did you misread the question (tests can use tricky wording)? Did you forget the information? Or was it something you hadn't learned? Go back and study any shaky areas that the practice tests reveal.

Taking these tests not only helps with your grade, but also aids in combating test anxiety. If you're already used to the test conditions, you're less likely to worry about it, and working through tests until you're scoring well gives you a confidence boost. Go through the practice tests until you feel comfortable, and then you can go into the test knowing that you're ready for it.

Test Tips

On test day, you should be confident, knowing that you've prepared well and are ready to answer the questions. But aside from preparation, there are several test day strategies you can employ to maximize your performance.

First, as stated before, get a good night's sleep the night before the test (and for several nights before that, if possible). Go into the test with a fresh, alert mind rather than staying up late to study.

Try not to change too much about your normal routine on the day of the test. It's important to eat a nutritious breakfast, but if you normally don't eat breakfast at all, consider eating just a protein bar. If you're a coffee drinker, go ahead and have your normal coffee. Just make sure you time it so that the caffeine doesn't wear off right in the middle of your test. Avoid sugary beverages, and drink enough water to stay hydrated but not so much that you need a restroom break 10 minutes into the test. If your test isn't first thing in the morning, consider going for a walk or doing a light workout before the test to get your blood flowing.

Allow yourself enough time to get ready, and leave for the test with plenty of time to spare so you won't have the anxiety of scrambling to arrive in time. Another reason to be early is to select a good seat. It's helpful to sit away from doors and windows, which can be distracting. Find a good seat, get out your supplies, and settle your mind before the test begins.

When the test begins, start by going over the instructions carefully, even if you already know what to expect. Make sure you avoid any careless mistakes by following the directions.

Then begin working through the questions, pacing yourself as you've practiced. If you're not sure on an answer, don't spend too much time on it, and don't let it shake your confidence. Either skip it and come back later, or eliminate as many wrong answers as possible and guess among the remaining ones. Don't dwell on these questions as you continue—put them out of your mind and focus on what lies ahead.

Be sure to read all of the answer choices, even if you're sure the first one is the right answer. Sometimes you'll find a better one if you keep reading. But don't second-guess yourself if you do immediately know the answer. Your gut instinct is usually right. Don't let test anxiety rob you of the information you know.

If you have time at the end of the test (and if the test format allows), go back and review your answers. Be cautious about changing any, since your first instinct tends to be correct, but make sure you didn't misread any of the questions or accidentally mark the wrong answer choice. Look over any you skipped and make an educated guess.

At the end, leave the test feeling confident. You've done your best, so don't waste time worrying about your performance or wishing you could change anything. Instead, celebrate the successful completion of this test. And finally, use this test to learn how to deal with anxiety even better next time.

Review Video: Test Anxiety
Visit mometrix.com/academy and enter code: 100340

Important Qualification

Not all anxiety is created equal. If your test anxiety is causing major issues in your life beyond the classroom or testing center, or if you are experiencing troubling physical symptoms related to your anxiety, it may be a sign of a serious physiological or psychological condition. If this sounds like your situation, we strongly encourage you to seek professional help.

Online Resources

Due to our efforts to try to keep this book to a manageable length, we've created a link that will give you access to all of your online resources:

mometrix.com/resources719/cpabusenvcon

It's Your Moment, Let's Celebrate It!

Share your story @mometrixtestpreparation